Golden's Journal

20 Sampler Blocks Honoring Prairie Farm Life

By
**Christina DeArmond,
Eula Lang and Kaye Spitzli**

Golden's Journal

20 SAMPLER BLOCKS HONORING PRAIRIE FARM LIFE

By Christina DeArmond, Eula Lang and Kaye Spitzli

Editor: Deb Rowden
Designer: Brian Grubb
Photography: Aaron T. Leimkuehler
Illustration: Lon Eric Craven
Technical Editor: Barbara Nesemeyer
Production assistance: Jo Ann Groves

Published by:
Kansas City Star Books
1729 Grand Blvd.
Kansas City, Missouri, 64108 USA

First edition, first printing ISBN: 978-1-933466-36-1

Library of Congress Control Number: 2007937629

Printed in the United States of America by
Walsworth Publishing Co., Marceline, MO

To order copies, call StarInfo at (816) 234-4636 and say "Books."

KANSAS CITY STAR BOOKS
Kansas City, Missouri

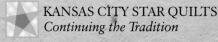
KANSAS CITY STAR QUILTS
Continuing the Tradition

PickleDish.com
The Quilter's Home Page

www.PickleDish.com

Contents

Dedication

We dedicate this book in honor of our grandmothers who passed on to us a legacy of family, love and quilts. Also, to our mothers Arlene Westerhouse Lawson, Elizabeth Finley Slankard and Mary Irene Jobe Scranton who lovingly carried on the tradition. We desire to pass it on to the next generation, our daughters and daughters-in-law: Jamie, Jacque, Brianne, Elizabeth, Breezy, Jenny and Morgan. May you continue being wrapped in the love and warmth of family—and quilts.

Acknowledgements

We gratefully thank all those who have been instrumental in helping us bring this book from concept to reality.

Doug Weaver for taking a chance on the three of us.

Deb Rowden for guiding, teaching and prodding us on to completion.

Brian Grubb for the beautiful design and extra work on the map.

Photographer Aaron T. Leimkuehler who was such a joy to watch and work with.

Additional Star staff who took our ideas and made them look good: especially Barbara Nesemeyer, Lon Eric Craven and Jo Ann Groves.

Arlene Lawson for sharing memories and her marvelous pictures, and for making quilts and sewing down lots of binding.

Our wonderful staff at Quilting Bits & Pieces in Eudora, Kansas for taking up the slack as we worked on the book. Special thanks to Nan Doljac, Peggy Claggett, Reeze Hanson, Amber Smith and Shannon Slagle who also made projects for the book.

The Bits & Pieces Wednesday morning Bible study ladies for encouragement, prayers and friendship.

Karen Gerecke, Carol Barry, Deb Gudenkauf and Janet Blessing for loaning us their beautiful quilts. Also, Stoney Point Church, Vinland, Kansas, for a photo.

Arlene Westerhouse Lawson, Golden's daughter, still loves to quilt.

Foreword

My grandmother, Leoti Golden Milburn Westerhouse, was a great storyteller and we, her grandchildren, loved hearing her stories. She kept diaries for many years. In 1976, inspired by the Bicentennial, I asked her to write a journal of her memories. I wish I had thought to ask about many other things, but I am very thankful for these preserved words in her handwriting.

As a child I was intrigued with her middle name, as I never knew anyone else with that name – Goldie, Golda, but not Golden. So when we started putting this journal into quilt patterns, this was the name we chose to use. Later, I was told that Grandma never really liked her middle name!

Grandma loved to sew and passed this love on to my mother and also to me. I grew up sleeping under her quilts, some quilted and some tied, all of which contained fabrics from the scrapbag. Each block of fabric could be identified as "my blue dress, mom's blouse, Peggy's sundress, grandma's apron." My prayer is that this series is a worthy tribute to a wonderful woman who was also a quilter and historian. I am so proud to be a part of her family.

— Kaye Spitzli
June, 2007
Eudora, Kansas

Grandchildren Kenny and Kaye and kittens at Golden's farm in 1950. Grandma's chicken house is in the background.

Leoti Golden Milburn

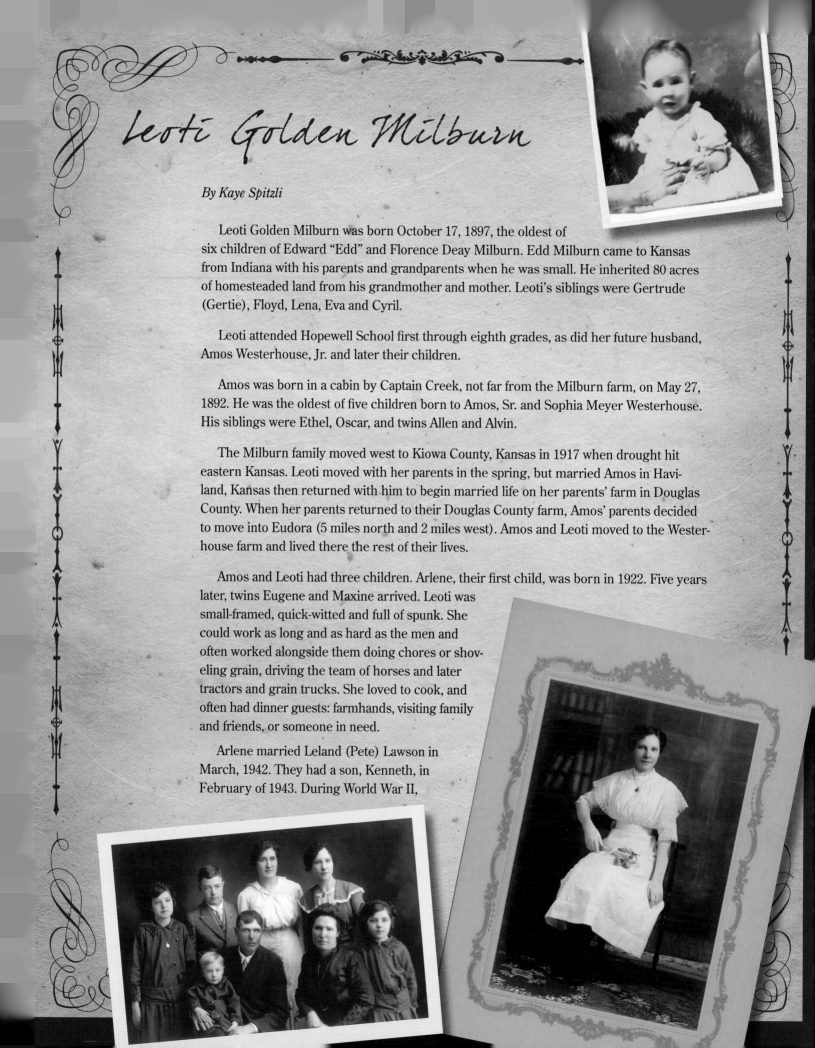

By Kaye Spitzli

Leoti Golden Milburn was born October 17, 1897, the oldest of six children of Edward "Edd" and Florence Deay Milburn. Edd Milburn came to Kansas from Indiana with his parents and grandparents when he was small. He inherited 80 acres of homesteaded land from his grandmother and mother. Leoti's siblings were Gertrude (Gertie), Floyd, Lena, Eva and Cyril.

Leoti attended Hopewell School first through eighth grades, as did her future husband, Amos Westerhouse, Jr. and later their children.

Amos was born in a cabin by Captain Creek, not far from the Milburn farm, on May 27, 1892. He was the oldest of five children born to Amos, Sr. and Sophia Meyer Westerhouse. His siblings were Ethel, Oscar, and twins Allen and Alvin.

The Milburn family moved west to Kiowa County, Kansas in 1917 when drought hit eastern Kansas. Leoti moved with her parents in the spring, but married Amos in Haviland, Kansas then returned with him to begin married life on her parents' farm in Douglas County. When her parents returned to their Douglas County farm, Amos' parents decided to move into Eudora (5 miles north and 2 miles west). Amos and Leoti moved to the Westerhouse farm and lived there the rest of their lives.

Amos and Leoti had three children. Arlene, their first child, was born in 1922. Five years later, twins Eugene and Maxine arrived. Leoti was small-framed, quick-witted and full of spunk. She could work as long and as hard as the men and often worked alongside them doing chores or shoveling grain, driving the team of horses and later tractors and grain trucks. She loved to cook, and often had dinner guests: farmhands, visiting family and friends, or someone in need.

Arlene married Leland (Pete) Lawson in March, 1942. They had a son, Kenneth, in February of 1943. During World War II,

Pete was sent to active duty in the South Pacific. In 1944, Arlene and Kenny moved back to the farm while Pete was overseas. The twins, Eugene and Maxine, were seniors in high school.

When Sunflower Ordinance Plant opened in 1945, many people relocated to the Eudora/DeSoto area. There wasn't sufficient housing for the influx of workers and rooms were rented in private homes. With the plant's back gate just a few miles from the farm, Amos and Leoti rented out their smoke house to one man. A small room in the front of the garage housed another man, as did the milk house. A couple stayed in the 'front room' and another couple with a baby rented Amos and Leoti's bedroom. Leoti and Arlene cooked meals for everyone. Then, to 'do her part' for the country, Leoti applied for a job at the Sunflower plant. Despite having only an eighth grade education, entrance test results qualified her for a supervisor job that required a college degree. She worked nights at the plant while she cooked and kept up the house, garden and chickens during the day. She often took eggs and dressed chickens to sell at work.

Clockwise from top: Leoti Golden Milburn; Amos's family and the Captain Creek cabin (Amos is riding the tricycle on the right); Golden's 8th grade graduation; Leoti (back right) with her family.

Leoti continued to raise chickens until the late 1980s. Known as the 'egg lady', she peddled eggs to regular Eudora customers every Saturday morning.

She taught Sunday School for many years, beginning with preschoolers in the "cradle roll class" and then the Fidelis adult class at Eudora Methodist Church. An active church member, she held office in the women's society meetings, as well as her local "club", the (HDU) or Home Demonstration Unit.

Leoti received a diary for her 54th birthday in October, 1951 and wrote daily until her eyesight no longer allowed it. Her diaries are full of news of everyday farm life. She recorded rain amounts and temperature; which field the 'menfolk' worked in, or the price of wheat, corn, or soy beans at the market. She noted bills paid and their amount: "Got our electric card today - $4.57. Had a 'scoldy' letter from Aunt Ida which I richly deserved." Another entry stated she had a busy day: got up a bit early to get the chores done and the brooder house cleaned out, then made cinnamon rolls and got to the circle meeting at church by 8:30 a.m.

Tucked inside her diaries are a few letters, now and then a newspaper clipping, usually of a humorous bent. One diary has a letter stuffed inside from the Topeka, Kansas Mission, thanking her for 30 quilts she sent for the needy. Besides making quilts for missions and the nursing home, she knitted booties and caps and made clothing for children on Indian reservations in Arizona and North Dakota.

Son Eugene married the pastor's daughter, Dorothy Willard. They rented a farm home in the area and continued to farm with Amos. Eugene and Dorothy moved to the Milburn farm in the 1950s. They have three children: Peggy, Mike and Bill. Twin Maxine married Arvon Gale Gerstenberger in the Captain Creek Church. Gale's pharmacy career took them to El Dorado, Mulvane, McPherson, Newton and Hutchinson, Kansas. They have two children, Greg and Patty.

Pete came home from the South Pacific in 1945 and Kaye was born in 1946. Arlene and Pete moved to Eudora in 1947.

Amos and Leoti's seven grandchildren visited often. The farm was an exciting place for a grandchild to visit, and we spent many weekends there. We have great memories of helping with the chores and floating our 2 x 4 boats in the cow tank. Grandma always had a fresh-baked pie or cinnamon rolls. The three siblings are close and often went to card parties or dances together, leaving Grandma with all the grandchildren. These events are all noted in her diary, some more positively than others.

Leoti regularly visited our homes. Many diary entries tell of spending the afternoon helping a daughter or daughter-in-law get caught up with the laundry or ironing, or just sewing together at one home or another.

Leoti always called Amos "Daddy" and refers to him that way in her diaries. He called her "Mommy" unless there was work to be done outside: then she was "George". They worked side by side for all 67 years of their married life.

Amos died on July 9, 1982 at the age of 90. Leoti continued to live at the farm and kept her garden for many years. She went to live with Arlene and Pete at age 96 and died November 6, 1994 at the age of 97. Their lives continue to be an inspiration to all who knew them.

Amos and Leoti's last fall walk in the timber.

Hopewell Farm and Community

The original Hopewell farm is located between the Milburn and Westerhouse farms, just west of the Johnson/Douglas county line, south of Eudora, Kansas.

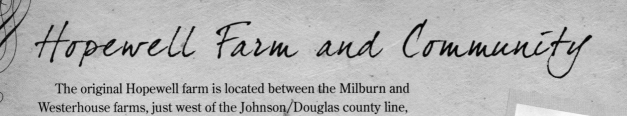

The name of Hopewell came with early settlers. As the story goes, they hoped to find land where there was water for a good well and they did. Grandpa used to say there was an underground river there and the wells on both the Hopewell farm and the Westerhouse farm had lots of water, even in very dry years. The original farm was recently purchased from Paul and Jean Gabriel by longtime community resident Richard Knabe, who is dedicated to preserving the history of Hopewell. It's becoming a place where people can gather together and share memories and history of the Hopewell community.

A volunteer group of neighbors, former neighbors, and others was formed by Richard and Linda Knabe in 2003. The group meets several times a year at the farm. They have put up and painted fences. Work on a wood frame barn held together with wood pegs continues. A windmill is in the plans to be placed where the old one stood. Their goals are to involve more community members in work days and activities at Hopewell, and to relocate the church building and school house to the Hopewell farm.

Depending on the season, they thresh wheat and oats, cut loose hay and store it in a portable barn, pick and shell ear corn, raise flax, and make hollyhock dolls and seed pictures. Longtime residents tell stories of ancestors arriving in the area, and share collected pictures and stories of the area history. One workday/demonstration included a chuck wagon dinner, followed with homemade ice cream. Some meetings have even featured singing songs from old Hopewell school books.

Clockwise from top: Hopewell farm, threshing activities at a fall 2006 community gathering. Eugene is standing in the truck bed, right. (photos by Ray Rowden)

Basic Sewing Instructions

These guidelines will be used in all the projects in this book unless otherwise noted.

CUTTING

Our fabric requirements are for fabric that is approximately 42" wide. Before cutting, we recommend pre-washing fabric to prevent dye from bleeding. This will also make for uniform shrinkage once the quilt is completed and washed.

Sharp rotary blades are important for nice, clean cuts. It is also easier to cut fabric when using rulers that have grids on the bottom so they do not slide. The more precisely pieces are cut, the easier they will be to match up, which will make for a more precise finished block.

SEWING

Always sew with the right sides of the fabric together. Use a precise ¼" seam allowance. If the seam allowance is off even a little, it can make a big difference in the finished size of the block. Follow the assembly instructions for each block to get the block to fit together correctly.

MITERING CORNERS

Some blocks have pieces that fit together by mitering the corners. This is actually very easy to do and has a nice finished look. To achieve this, it is important to mark the point where the two seam lines intersect.

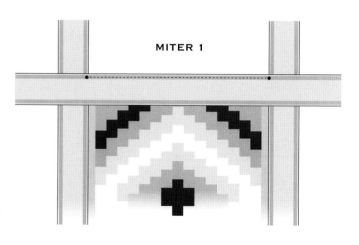

Once the points are marked on the two pieces that are to be sewn together, pin the seam lines together so the points line up and do not shift as you move the fabric to the machine. Mark a line using a 45° angle.

Lower the machine needle exactly into the point and take two stitches forward. Reverse for two stitches to lock these stitches in place. Now, sew from the point to the end of the seam line. Repeat this process for the seam that intersects this point, but goes in the other direction. Trim seam allowances to ¼" and press open.

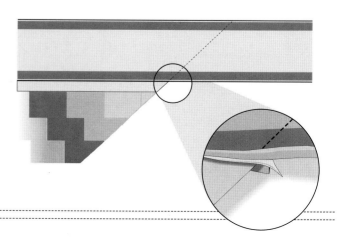

PRESSING

The general rule is to always press towards the darker fabric. Now and then, it is awkward to do this; if so, it is fine to press to the lighter side. It is **very important** to press seams as you go. The block pieces will fit together more precisely.

BORDERS

When adding borders, it is important to measure the quilt instead of just adding strips to the sides or assuming your quilt measures the same as the one in the book. For the border to fit correctly, measure the quilt in two or three spots and then cut your border strips to the average of these measurements. This will prevent "wavy" borders or quilts where the middle is larger than the borders.

EMBROIDERY

The embroidery on the 30s version of Golden's Journal border (see page 117) and on the flour sack tea towel (see page 103) is done using the stem stitch. This is probably the most common embroidery stitch. The other stitch we used is French knots. Use 2 strands of embroidery floss or 1 strand of perle cotton, size 16. It is fun to use variegated floss or perle cotton for a pleasing look. We recommend a size 7 crewel embroidery needle for easy threading. It is important to use an embroidery hoop so the design does not get distorted as you work on it.

STEM STITCH

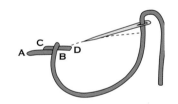

1. Make a small "quilter's knot" at the end of floss.

2. Working from left to right, bring the needle up at A.

3. While holding down floss with your left thumb, put the needle down at B and up at C.

4. Continue holding down the floss with your left thumb, put needle down at D and up just in front of B.

5. Repeat to the end of the line.
   Make each stitch about the same length, and begin halfway along the previous stitch. It is easier to go around curves by slightly reducing the stitch length. Always make sure to hold the thread down so that the stitch is above the thread.

FRENCH KNOTS

1. Knot end of floss.

2. Bring thread up at the desired point.

3. Holding thread taut with the forefinger and thumb of your left hand, wrap the thread tightly around the tip of the needle twice.

4. While still holding the thread next to the fabric, insert the needle very close to the point and pull the needle through to the back of the work so that the knot lies neatly on top of the fabric.

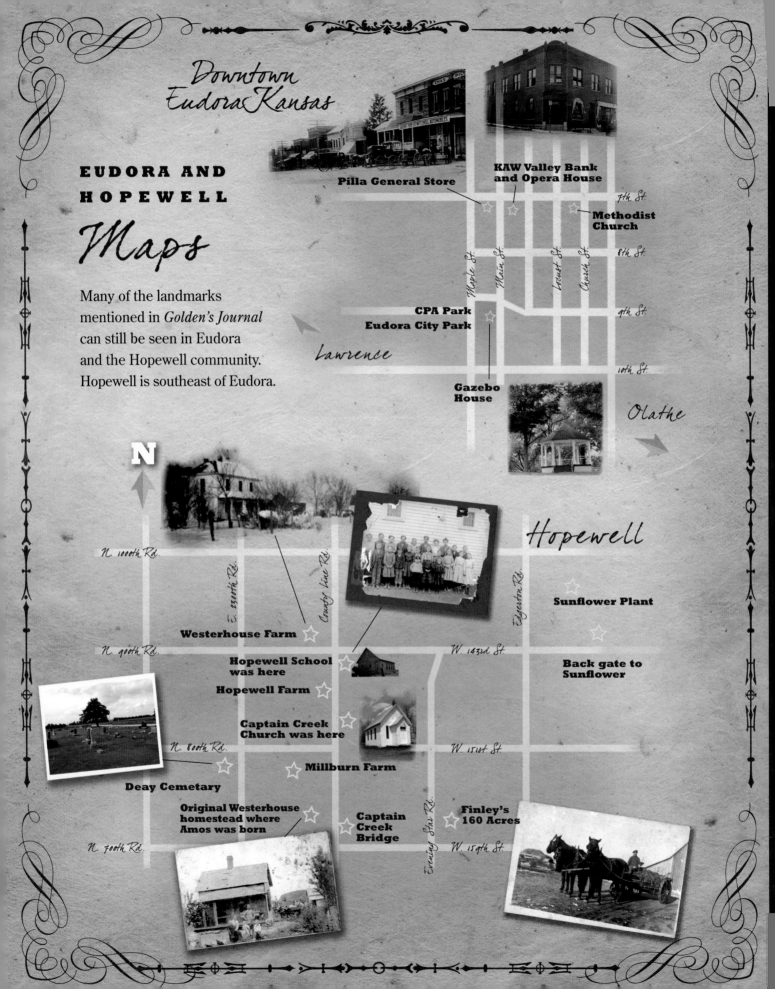

Downtown Eudora Kansas

EUDORA AND HOPEWELL

Maps

Many of the landmarks mentioned in *Golden's Journal* can still be seen in Eudora and the Hopewell community. Hopewell is southeast of Eudora.

Pilla General Store

KAW Valley Bank and Opera House

Methodist Church

7th St.

8th St.

Maple St.

Main St.

Locust St.

Church St.

CPA Park
Eudora City Park

9th St.

Lawrence

10th St.

Gazebo House

Olathe

N

N. 1000th Rd.

E. 2300th Rd.

County Line Rd.

Edgerton Rd.

Hopewell

Sunflower Plant

Westerhouse Farm

N. 900th Rd.

W. 143rd St.

Hopewell School was here

Back gate to Sunflower

Hopewell Farm

Captain Creek Church was here

W. 151st St.

N. 800th Rd.

Millburn Farm

Deay Cemetary

Original Westerhouse homestead where Amos was born

N. 700th Rd.

Captain Creek Bridge

Evening Star Rd.

Finley's 160 Acres

W. 159th St.

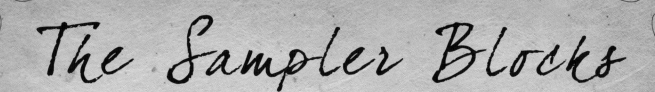

The Sampler Blocks

All blocks finish to 9".
The block order journal entries
follow events in Golden's life ....

SANTA FE TRAIL

CABIN WINDOWS

KANSAS TROUBLES

BRIDLE PATH

SCHOOL GIRL'S PUZZLE

MERRY-GO-ROUND

STEPS TO THE ALTAR

CORN AND BEANS

RED CROSS

FARMER'S FIELDS

HENS AND CHICKENS

PIG PEN

FARMER'S DAUGHTER

OLD COUNTRY CHURCH

GRANDMOTHER'S FLOWER GARDEN

SCHOOLHOUSE

SUNFLOWER

SNOWBALL

TREE OF LIFE

BASKET

Patterns published by Hearth and Home

Santa Fe Trail

FROM GOLDEN'S JOURNAL

"My father, Ed Milburn was born in Lapel, Indiana in 1873. When he was a small boy, he came with his parents, Nancy Jane and Henry Milburn and grandparents, Kathryn and Jacob Huntzinger to Kansas. They homesteaded a section of land near the wagon trail. Eighty acres of this land is still in the family and has been for six generations, from Grandmother Huntzinger to their oldest of four daughters, Nancy Jane Milburn, Edd Milburn, me, now Eugene (my son) lives there and his youngest son, Bill lives on some of that acreage. The ruts of the wagon trail can still be seen through the pasture land."

The family of Golden's papa around 1887: Jim, Grandma Nancy Jane Milburn, Jake, Zue, Ike, Addie and Papa (Edd). Grandpa Henry Milburn died when Jim was 6 or 8 years old.

WAGON RUTS CARVED IN PRAIRIE SOD

The Santa Fe trail originated in 1821 when William Becknell left Franklin, Missouri, to trade "to the westward," and encountered a group of Mexican soldiers who guided them to Santa Fe, NM.

Westward trails began in various Missouri river towns: Old Franklin, New Franklin, Arrow Rock and Booneville among the earliest. Supplies and cargo could be unloaded from St. Louis steamboats and placed in freight wagons. Over time, the Santa Fe, Oregon and California Trails developed many routes, braids and shortcuts that varied due to landscapes and local conditions. Sometimes they joined or crossed, particularly at river and creek crossings.

Stagecoach and mail traffic began in the 1850s. With the building of the railroad to Santa Fe in 1880, the trail was largely abandoned. Of the 1,203 miles of trail route between Old Franklin, Missouri, and Santa Fe, New Mexico, more than 200 miles of ruts and trace remain visible; some 30 miles of these are protected on federal lands.

As we study the westward trails today, we believe the trail ruts left on Golden's land might belong to the California/Oregon Trail. These trails all came together and intertwined in this area, but it appears that the Santa Fe Trail is further south.

These ruts are still visible today on the Milburn farm.

HOW TO MAKE SANTA FE TRAIL

FABRIC REQUIREMENTS

CREAM PRINT: ¼ YARD

BLUE PRINT: **4" x 15"**

GREEN PRINT: **5" x 5"**

CUTTING INSTRUCTIONS

FROM THE BACKGROUND PRINT:

4 - 3 ½" squares.

12 - 2 ¾" squares cut in half diagonally twice to make a total of 48 quarter-square triangles.

4 - 1 ½" squares.

FROM THE GREEN PRINT:

5 - 1 ½" squares.

FROM THE BLUE PRINT:

4 - 2 ¾" squares cut in half diagonally twice to make a total of 16 quarter-square triangles.

Block Diagram

BLOCK ASSEMBLY

1. Make a nine-patch block. Sew the 1 ½" squares into rows of 3 squares each: 2 rows of green-cream-green (row A) and 1 row of cream-green-cream (row B). Press the seams toward the dark fabric. Sew the rows together with row B between the 2 row A's. Press seams.

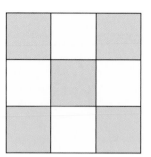

2. Sew the 16 blue and 16 of the cream quarter-square triangles into pairs along the long side of each triangle. Press the seams toward the dark fabric. You now have 16 squares that are half blue, half cream.

3. Sew 4 of these squares together with all 4 cream triangles toward the center of the block to form a blue around cream square-in-a-square unit. Press seams. Repeat to make 4 square-in-a-square units.

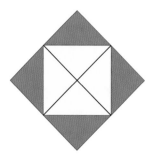

4. Sew the remaining cream triangles together in pairs along a short side. Press seams.

5. Sew 1 pair to each side of a square-in-a-square unit. Sew opposite sides, press seams, then the remaining sides, press seams. Repeat with the remaining 3 square-in-a-square units.

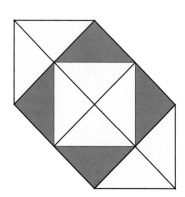

6. Assemble the blocks into rows.

Row 1: 3 ½" cream square, square-in-a-square unit, 3 ½" cream square.

Row 2: Square-in-a-square unit, nine-patch, square-in-a-square unit.

Row 3: 3 ½" cream square, square-in-a-square unit, 3 ½" cream square.

Press seams. Sew rows together. Press seams.

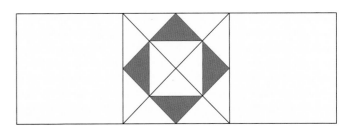

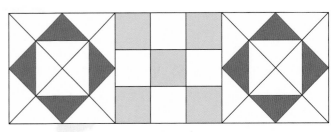

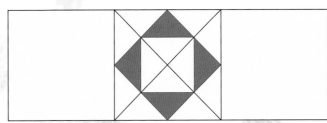

Pattern published by The Kansas City Star, April 17, 1940

Cabin Windows

FROM GOLDEN'S JOURNAL

"My home place is across the road east of the Deay Cemetery. Grandmother Nancy Jane inherited the 80 acres where Eugene lives.

I was born in a one room cabin. When I was about 2 years old, my dad, Edd Milburn, had the 4 room house built. It had two rooms down and two upstairs. Later he built on the east rooms, one down and one upstairs."

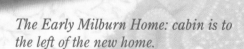

The Early Milburn Home: cabin is to the left of the new home.

HOW TO MAKE CABIN WINDOWS

FABRIC REQUIREMENTS

CREAM PRINT–BACKGROUND: ¹/₈ YARD

4 DIFFERENT BLUE PRINTS: ¹/₈ YARD EACH

CUTTING INSTRUCTIONS

CREAM PRINT:

16 – 1 ¼" squares
4 – 3 ⅛" squares

**DARKEST BLUE PRINT
(FOR SETTING TRIANGLES):**

4 – 3 ⅛" squares, cut in half diagonally
to make 8 triangles

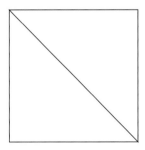

**TWO BLUE PRINTS
(FOR SMALL WINDOW UNITS):**

4 – 1 ¼" squares of each - 8 squares total
2 – 2 ¾" x 1 ¼" rectangles of each - 4 rectangles total

BLUE PRINT (FOR LARGE WINDOW UNIT):

1 – 6 ¾" x 1 ½" rectangle
2 – 3 ⅛" x 1 ½" rectangles

Sew the 1 ¼" squares together in sets of 3, alternating cream, blue, cream.

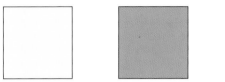

Make 4 sets of 3 from each of the 2 sets of fabric, 8 sets total. Press the seams toward the dark fabric.

BLOCK ASSEMBLY

Assemble as shown:

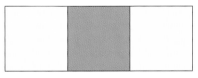

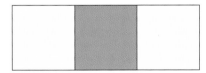

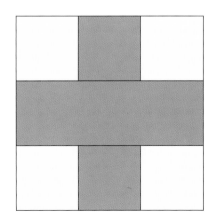

1. The top and bottom rows are matching sets of 3 squares. The middle row is one of the matching 2 ¾" x 1 ¼" blue print rectangles. Press the seams toward the center rectangle. Repeat with the other 3 pairs of 3 squares and 3 matching rectangles. You now have 4 Small Window units, 2 of each print.

BLOCK ASSEMBLY CONT.

2. Sew a 3 $\frac{1}{8}$" cream square to both sides of a 1 $\frac{1}{2}$" x 3 $\frac{1}{8}$" blue strip. Press the seams toward the blue fabric. Repeat. You now have 2 strip sets of: cream square, blue rectangle, cream square. Sew 1 strip set to each side of the 6 $\frac{3}{4}$" blue strip in as shown. Press seams toward the blue strip. This is your Large Window unit.

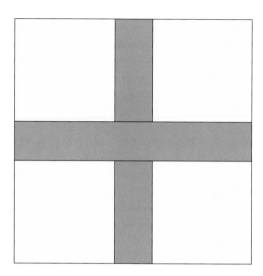

3. Sew 2 setting triangles to each small window unit along a short side of each triangle matching the square corner of the triangle to the window unit corner. This unit will form a larger triangle. (Refer to the block diagram and watch that your cross bars stay horizontal). Press the seams toward the window units. Repeat 3 more times. You now have 4 corner triangle units. Sew 1 unit to each side of the Large Window unit alternating the two prints. Press seams towards the Corner Triangles.

By Debbie Gudenkauf 2006

Pattern published by The Kansas City Star, 1934

Kansas Troubles

FROM GOLDEN'S JOURNAL

"Life was never easy. Amos' grandfather, Peter Westerhouse arrived from Prussia in 1848. He enlisted in the Home Guard on July 6, 1861, was wounded and taken prisoner at Lexington. He died at 47 in 1876 and is buried in the Deay Cemetery. Grandma Anna was left to raise the eight children and work the land. She eventually lost the land when she moved to town for fear of the Indians, who came through at night to steal tools and supplies. Amos was born in a three room house along side Captain Creek on this land. Many times the creek would flood and his family would move further up into the section to his grandmother's home.

When I was six I remember going to Lawrence with Papa and looking towards North Lawrence all underwater from the flooding Kaw River in 1903. In 1951 we hurried to Wilder, Kansas (near Bonner Springs) in the night to move my sister Lena, her family and our Mama who lived with them. We had hoped to arrive ahead of the flooding river, but by the time we got there, the family had fled further up the hill with the few things they could carry. The men went back to the house and carried everything they could up to the second floor—all to no avail as the water reached that level too."

The Westerhouse family at the three-room house along Captain Creek, about 1897. Ethel, Sophia (Mama), Oscar, Amos Sr. (Papa) and Amos Jr.

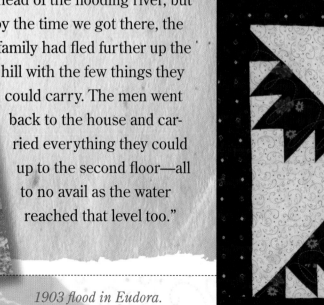

1903 flood in Eudora.

HOW TO MAKE KANSAS TROUBLES

FABRIC REQUIREMENTS

NEUTRAL SHIRTING: 11" x 14"

PLUM PRINT: 11" x 14"

CUTTING INSTRUCTIONS

FROM THE NEUTRAL SHIRTING:

Two 5 $\frac{3}{8}$" squares then cut once diagonally to make 4 half-square triangles.

Four 1 $\frac{5}{8}$" squares.

Eight 2" squares cut once diagonally to make 16 half-square triangles.

OR you may want to use 1.25" *Thangles* (see Resources on page 127).

FROM THE PLUM PRINT:

Twelve 2" squares cut once diagonally to make 24 half-square triangles,

OR strips wider than the *Thangles* sheet, plus 8 additional half-square triangles for the corners of each unit.

Two 3 $\frac{1}{8}$" squares cut once diagonally to make 4 half-square triangles.

BLOCK ASSEMBLY

1. Pair a neutral 2" triangle with a plum 2" triangle, right sides together. Sew along the long side. Press the seam toward the plum fabric. Repeat with the remaining triangles. Makes 16 square units or 1.25" *Thangles*.

2. If you used *Thangles*, trim the half-square triangles to 1 $\frac{5}{8}$".

3. Stitch 2 half-square triangle blocks together. Press seam to the dark side.

A

B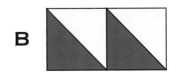

Repeat to make 8 units (4 A and 4 B).

BLOCK ASSEMBLY CONT.

4. Add 1 plum print half-square triangle to each of 4 of the units (unit A).

5. Add one 1 ⅝" square to the square end of each of the 4 B units.

6. Add 1 plum print half-square triangle to the other 4 units (unit B).

7. Sew the larger plum print half-square triangle to each of the 4 A units.

8. Sew the B units to each of the 4 A units.

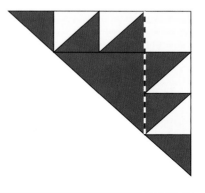

9. Sew the large shirting half-square triangle to the completed units.

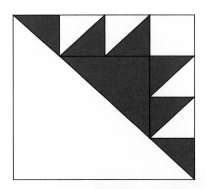

10. Sew the 4 units together.

Pattern published by The Kansas City Star, 1935

Bridle Path

FROM GOLDEN'S JOURNAL

"I always loved to ride and Papa was proud of my skill as a rider. As children, my sister Gertie and I would often race our horses up the lane and back to see who could win. What a joy it has been to see my grandchildren race their bicycles up and back this same lane.

Papa had a side-saddle in the barn; I'm not sure just when or where he acquired it but I was fascinated with it. One day I decided I would look very elegant riding around the mile section using the side saddle. Naturally this course would take me right past the Westerhouse farm. All went as I had imagined until I got just in front of their home and my horse spooked, tipping me off into the muddy ditch. I never knew if any of them witnessed my humiliation or not and never wanted to ask!"

Amos and Golden with horse and colt on June 24, 1917, just months before their wedding.

HOW TO MAKE BRIDLE PATH

FABRIC REQUIREMENTS

LIGHT GOLD: 8" SQUARE

DARK GOLD: 8" SQUARE

GOLD STRIPE: 5" x 24"

DARK BLUE: 4" x 8"

LIGHT BLUE: 5" x 24"

PURPLE PRINT: FAT-EIGHTH (11" x 18")

CUTTING INSTRUCTIONS

FROM THE DARK GOLD FABRIC:

8 - 1 ¼" squares.

2 - 3 ⅛" squares cut in half diagonally to make a total of 4 half-square triangles.

FROM THE LIGHT GOLD FABRIC:

8 - 1 ¼" squares.

2 - 3 ⅛" squares cut in half diagonally to make a total of 4 half-square triangles.

FROM THE DARK BLUE PRINT:

8 - 1 ¼" squares.

FROM THE PURPLE PRINT:

12 - 1 ¼" squares.

4 - 3 ⅛" squares cut in half diagonally to make a total of 8 half-square triangles.

FROM THE GOLD STRIPE AND THE LIGHT BLUE PRINT FABRICS:

3 strips each 1 ¼" x 24".

BLOCK ASSEMBLY

1. Make 2 nine-patch blocks using the purple, dark gold, and dark blue 1 ¼" squares. Press seams as you sew.

   Row 1: purple, dark gold, purple.

   Row 2: dark gold, dark blue, dark gold.

   Row 3: purple, dark gold, dark blue.

   Press seams. Sew rows together. Press seams.

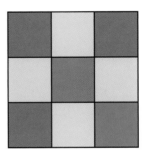

2. Make 2 nine-patch blocks using the purple, light gold, and dark blue 1 ¼" squares.

   Press seams as you sew.

   Row 1: purple, light gold, dark blue.

   Row 2: light gold, dark blue, light gold.

   Row 3: purple, light gold, purple.

   Press seams. Sew rows together. Press seams.

Gertie riding Gray Mare and Golden with Beauty.

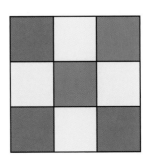

BLOCK ASSEMBLY CONT.

3. To make the 4 corner nine-patch blocks:
Sew 1 - 1 ¼" x 24" gold stripe strip inbetween
2 - 1 ¼" x 24" strips of light blue. Sew 1 - 1 ¼" x 24"
light blue strip inbetween 2 - 1 ¼" x 24" strips of
gold stripe. Press seams toward the light blue fabric.
Cross cut into 1 ¼" sections: Sew nine-patches
together – make 4.

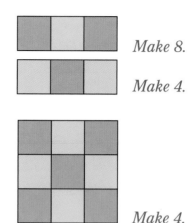

Make 8.

Make 4.

Make 4.

4. Pair a dark gold triangle with a purple triangle, right sides
together. Sew along the long side. Press the seam toward
the purple. Repeat with the remaining triangles so you have
4 dark gold/purple half-square triangles and 4 light gold/
purple half-square triangles.

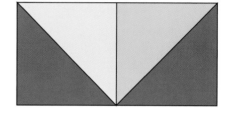

5. Assemble block
units as shown:

By Christina DeArmond, quilted by Eula Lang 2006

Pattern first published by Needlecraft Supply, a Chicago mail-order house for patterns, kits and fabric. Booklet: Patchwork Quilts and How to Make Them, 1938.

Schoolgirl's Puzzle

FROM GOLDEN'S JOURNAL

"All my brothers and sisters and I (Milburns) as well as the Westerhouses, and later our children, went to Hopewell school. Hopewell was a one-room building with a big heating stove in the back in which we burned coal. The coalhouse was back of the schoolhouse. Our water system was a water bucket with a dipper on a shelf in the corner of the room. When we were in school, there was no well on the school property so the water was carried from the nearest farm to the school. In nice weather we walked the 1 ½ miles to the school. In snowy weather my father would put the wagon box on big sled runners and put straw and blankets in the bottom, then take us to school picking up neighbor kids along the way.

Subjects we studied: reading, writing or penmanship, arithmetic, Kansas History, U.S. history or civil government, physiology, geography, spelling and grammar or English. We often had spelling matches and geography matches after last recess. These were a joy for me, especially the geography. Games we played were Blackman, Anti-over, Dare Base, Fox and Goose, Baseball - Shinny, and we walked on stilts."

East Hopewell School about 1905. Golden is in the dark dress directly above the sign. Amos is in the back row, second from right.

Another East Hopewell School photo, about 1907. Golden is second from left in middle row, Amos is fifth from the right in the back row.

HOW TO MAKE SCHOOLGIRL'S PUZZLE

FABRIC REQUIREMENTS

CREAM BACKGROUND: $^1/_8$ YARD

LARGE FLORAL PRINT: $^1/_8$ YARD

BURGUNDY PRINT: $^1/_8$ YARD

GREEN PRINT: $^1/_8$ YARD

CUTTING INSTRUCTIONS

Cream background: 5 – 3 $^1/_8$" squares.

Large floral print: 3 – 3 $^1/_8$" squares and 2 – 2 ¾" squares.

Burgundy print: 2 – 3 $^1/_8$" squares.

Green print: 4 – 2 ¾" squares.

BLOCK ASSEMBLY

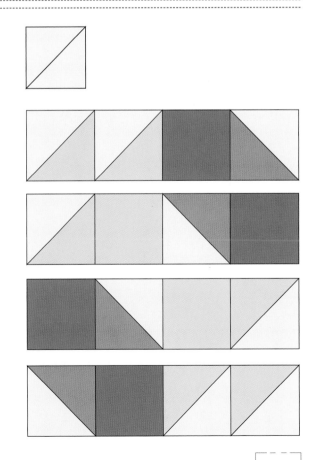

1. Draw a diagonal line from corner to corner on the wrong side of each 3 $^1/_8$" cream square. Place a cream square right sides together with a 3 $^1/_8$" large floral square. Stitch 1/4" away from each side of the drawn line, then cut apart on the diagonal line. This makes 2 half-square triangle units. Repeat this step with the other two sets of cream and large floral squares. Press the seams toward the darker fabric. You now have 6 cream/large floral half-square triangle units.

2. Repeat this process with the remaining 2 - 3 $^1/_8$" cream squares and the 2 - 3 $^1/_8$" burgundy squares. You now have 4 cream/burgundy half-square triangle units.

3. Assemble each row as shown below. Press the seams of the first and third rows to the right and the seams of the second and fourth rows to the left. Stitch the rows together as shown.

Pattern published by The Kansas City Star, 1935

Merry-Go-Round

FROM GOLDEN'S JOURNAL

"Amos and I had our first date at a CPA picnic*. We had gone to school together, but he seemed one of the older boys (he was 6 years older than me) so I knew he had some of the older girls expecting a date and was surprised and thrilled when he asked me out of a bunch of girls. We rode the merry-go-round all evening and it cost 5 cents a ride.

The next winter we had Thursday night dates as there was a continued movie on in Eudora in what was the Opera house** - upstairs over the corner building across from what is now the City hall. This was called the "Million Dollar Movie". (These were silent movies.)

Amos had a fancy horse and buggy which he got when he graduated from 8th grade. With our 'regular' dates, that horse soon learned the way to my house which gave us time for 'courting' on the way home. Then one time he asked another girl to go to the dance with him as she was a good dancer. Amos had to fight that horse all the way to her house as the horse wanted to come to my house."

Amos, age 23.

Amos Westerhouse, Jr. in 1915—a handsome catch.

HOW TO MAKE MERRY-GO-ROUND

FABRIC REQUIREMENTS

CREAM PRINT/NEUTRAL: ⅛ YARD
8 PRINTS: 8" SQUARE OF EACH
CENTER CIRCLE: 2" SQUARE

CUTTING INSTRUCTIONS

NOTE: Cut template pieces **individually,** right side of fabric up, or stack the fabric **right sides up** if cutting more than 1 at a time.

TEMPLATES A, B, C, AND D:

Cut 4 each of the neutral fabric.

TEMPLATES F, G, H AND I:

Cut 2 each of 2 different prints.

TEMPLATE K:

Cut 1 from the 2" square of fabric.

---

*   Eudora still observes an annual "CPA Picnic". The Central Protective Association was formed in 1901 for protection of its members and their property against cattle rustlers and horse thieves. Today its only function is the July carnival weekend. Early picnics included a basket dinner, parades, games and contests, speeches, and a merry-go-round. A dance was the highlight of the evening with music provided by locals.

**   The Opera house is now a private apartment above Madame Hatter's Tea Room on the SE corner of 7th and Main.

BLOCK ASSEMBLY

1. Following the block diagram, pair a neutral piece with the corresponding wedge of print fabric and sew right sides together. Press the seam toward the dark fabric. Sew the wedges together to form the block. Press. Appliqué the circle (template K) over the center of the block.

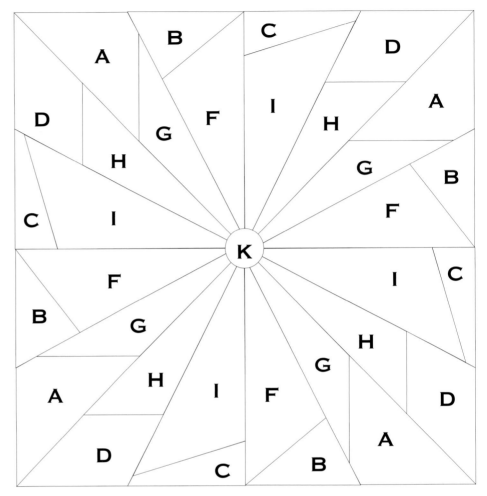

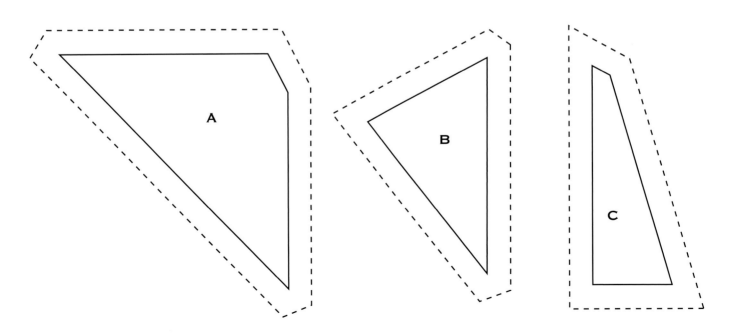

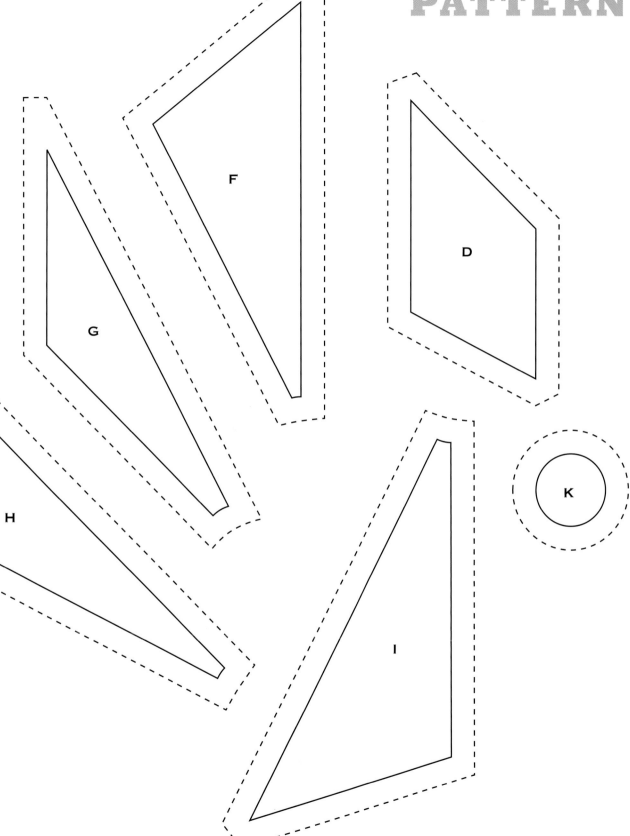

Merry-Go-Round
PATTERNS

F

D

G

H

K

I

Pattern published by Mrs. Danner in 1970. A mail-order pattern source known as *Mrs. Danner's Quilts* (ESTABLISHED 1934)

Steps to the Altar

FROM GOLDEN'S JOURNAL

"In 1916, eastern Kansas had a dry spell and by early spring it was too dry to plant. Papa's sister and family were living in Western Kansas where the outlook was much brighter. In March of 1917, my parents moved to Kiowa County, Kansas (near Haviland, Kansas).

I had received my diamond ring at Christmas 1916, but I went with the folks and lived there. Amos and I were married by the Methodist preacher on Friday, November 7, 1917 at my folk's home at Haviland. My four-year-old cousin, Mildred Arlene Griffin, was our flower girl.

The following Sunday afternoon friends and family came for a reception and photos were taken.

Little Mildred died in 1921 when she was just eight years old. In 1922, when our first born was a girl, we named her Arlene after Mildred Arlene."

The newlyweds

HOW TO MAKE STEPS TO THE ALTAR
FABRIC REQUIREMENTS

TAN PRINT: $^1/_8$ YARD

CREAM PRINT: $^1/_8$ YARD

BLUE PRINT: $^1/_8$ YARD

BROWN PRINT: $^1/_8$ YARD

RED PRINT: $^1/_8$ YARD

CUTTING INSTRUCTIONS

Tan print: 13 - 1 ½" squares.

Cream print: 20 - 1 ½" squares.

Blue print: 16 - 1 ½" squares.

Brown print: 12 - 1 ½" squares.

Red print: 20 - 1 ½" squares.

Amos and Golden with flower girl Mildred Arlene Griffin.

BLOCK ASSEMBLY

1. Sew the 1 ½" squares into rows.

Row 1: red, blue, tan, cream, red, cream, tan, blue, red.

Row 2: blue, tan, cream, red, brown, red, cream, tan, blue.

Row 3: tan, cream, red, brown, blue, brown, red, cream, tan.

Row 4: cream, red, brown, blue, cream, blue, brown, red, cream.

Row 5: red, brown, blue, cream, tan, cream, blue, brown, red.

Row 6: cream, red, brown, blue, cream, blue, brown, red, cream.

Row 7: tan, cream, red, brown, blue, brown, red, cream, tan.

Row 8: blue, tan, cream, red, brown, red, cream, tan, blue.

Row 9: red, blue, tan, cream, red, cream, tan, blue, red.

Press the seam allowances to the right on the odd numbered rows. Press the seam allowances to the left on the even numbered rows. Sew the rows together in order. Press seams.

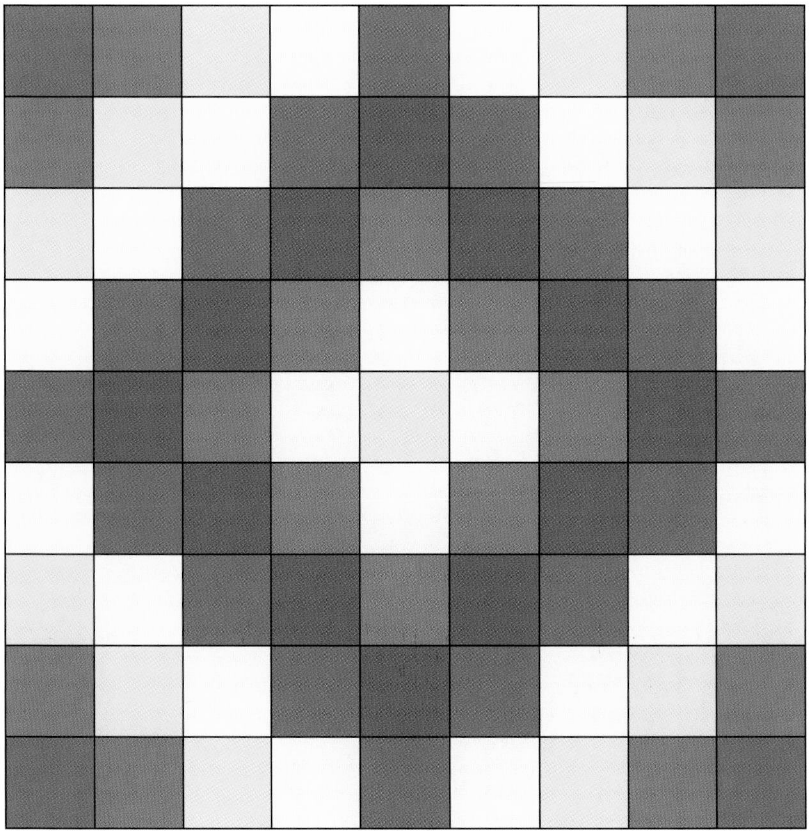

Pattern published by The Kansas City Star, 1930

Corn and Beans

FROM GOLDEN'S JOURNAL

"Our first 'Home' was a cook shack on wheels which we pulled into the middle of the cornfield, then moved to another field as each was picked. This was on corn land in Kiowa County, Kansas (near Haviland) in November of 1917. We helped my family pick corn and I cooked for the men. Most of the cooking and eating was done outside.

We bought a new 1918 Ford with the money we made from the corn picking."

Amos, standing by the fruits of his labor. Home was the cook shack on the right.

HOW TO MAKE CORN AND BEANS

FABRIC REQUIREMENTS

BACKGROUND: 1/8 YARD

4 PRINTS FOR CENTER SQUARE: 6" X 6" EACH

DARK BROWN PRINT: 6" X 6"

2 SMALL GREEN PRINTS: 5" X 5"

4 BROWN/GREEN FLORAL PRINTS: 5" X 5" EACH

CUTTING INSTRUCTIONS

FROM BACKGROUND FABRIC:

2 - 3 7/8" squares, cut in half diagonally to make 4 large A triangles.

10 - 2 3/8" squares, cut in half diagonally to make 20 small B triangles.

FROM 4 LARGE PRINTS FOR CENTER SQUARE:

1 - 3 7/8" square of each, cut in half diagonally to make 8 large A triangles. Use 4 of these, 1 of each color for the center triangles.

FROM DARK BROWN PRINT FABRIC:

3 - 2 3/8" squares, cut in half diagonally to make 6 small B triangles.

FROM 2 GREEN PRINT FABRICS:

2 - 2 3/8" squares of each green, cut in half diagonally to make 8 small B triangles. Use 3 of each color.

FROM 4 BROWN/GREEN FLORAL PRINTS:

1 - 4 1/4" square of each, cut in half diagonally twice to make 16 medium C triangles. Use one of each color for the flying geese units.

BLOCK ASSEMBLY

1. Lay out your cut triangles on a flat surface or design wall. This will help you decide on color placement.

BLOCK ASSEMBLY CONT.

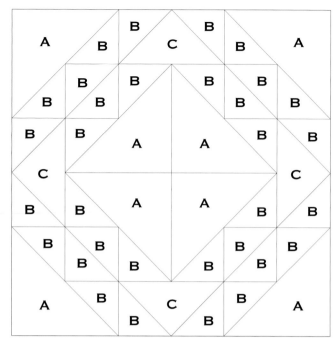

Block Diagram

2. Sew 1 small B background triangle to 1 small B dark triangle. Press the seam toward the dark fabric. Repeat 3 times to form 4 half-square triangle units as shown below.

3. Sew a small B background triangle to each side of the dark side of the square as shown below. This makes a triangle unit. Repeat with the remaining 3 half-square triangle units. Press the seams toward the dark fabric.

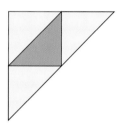

4. Sew one of these triangle units to 1 of the 4 center large A triangles as shown below. Repeat for all 4 sections of the center. Press 2 seams towards the background and 2 seams towards the dark prints. You now have 4 center square units.

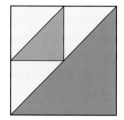

5. Sew two of the 4 center square units together along a long dark side. Repeat with the other 2 units. Press both seams the same way. Sew these 2 units together along the long dark sides, the center seams will lay in opposite directions. Press the seam to 1 side.

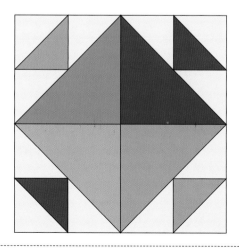

6. Sew 1 small B background triangle to each short side of a medium C print triangle forming a flying geese unit. Press the seam away from the darker print. Repeat with the other 3 medium C triangles. Press the seams toward the dark fabric. You now have 4 flying geese units.

7. Stitch the remaining small B print triangle to each side of the flying geese unit. Place the triangle so that one of the short sides extends out in a straight line from the long side of the geese triangle as shown. Press the seams toward the dark fabrics. Repeat with the other 3 flying geese units watching your color placement.

8. Sew 1 section to each side of the center square. Press the seams toward the geese units.

9. Sew the 4 large A background triangles to each corner. Press the seams toward the background triangles.

Pattern published by Coats & Clark, 1945

Red Cross

FROM GOLDEN'S JOURNAL

"In January 1918 we came to Amos' folks and later moved to my home place which had been closed up as my folks stayed in Haviland. Amos had planted wheat the fall before and had a good wheat crop. This caused him to be exempt from the draft of World War I until harvest. Of course, the war was over before he was called.

We bought cattle right away to put on the pasture land and several milking cows. Amos and I farmed the Milburn land as at that time his younger brothers were all still home and could help Amos' parents with the farm there.

When his brothers left home, Amos helped over there when his father needed him. By the time my parents returned to their farm, the Westerhouses moved to town. We then moved to the Westerhouse farm and farmed that land."

Amos Jr. ready to harvest.

HOW TO MAKE RED CROSS

FABRIC REQUIREMENTS

BACKGROUND: 8" x 22"
4 RED PRINTS: 6" x 6½" EACH

CUTTING INSTRUCTIONS

FROM THE BACKGROUND PRINT:

2 - 2" squares cut in half diagonally to make a total of 4 half-square triangles.

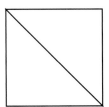

3 - 3 ½" squares cut in half diagonally twice to make a total of 12 quarter-square triangles.

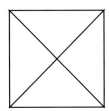

5 - 2 ⅛" squares.

FROM EACH OF THE 4 RED FABRICS:

2 - 2 ⅛" squares.

1 - 5 ¼" x 2 ⅛" rectangle.

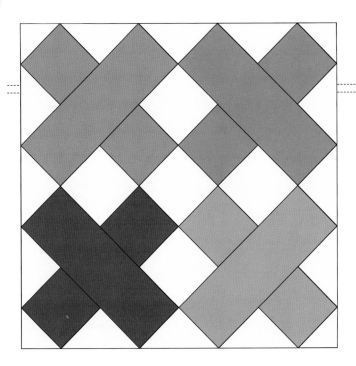

BLOCK ASSEMBLY

1. Using 5 - 2 ⅛" background squares and 1 of each 2 ⅛" red squares, make a nine-patch block. Press seams toward the dark fabrics when possible. This forms the center of your block.

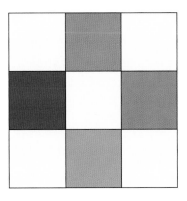

The family with a later harvest, August 1941.

45

BLOCK ASSEMBLY CONT.

2. Sew 1 quarter-square triangle to the opposite 2 sides of a red 2 ⅛" square. Press seams toward the dark fabric. Repeat with the remaining 3 red squares.

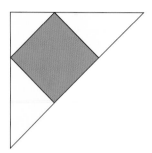

3. Sew 1 half-square triangle onto the third side of the 2 ⅛" square unit as shown above. This forms a triangle unit. Press seams toward the dark fabric. Repeat with the other 3 red square units.

4. Add the matching 5 ¼" rectangle to the fourth side of the red square in the triangle unit. Press seams toward the dark fabric. Repeat with the other three triangle units. Now you have 4 Y units.

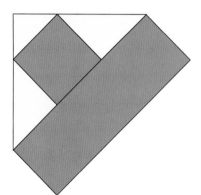

5. Sew 2 Y units to opposite sides of the center nine-patch, matching colors with the colored block in the nine-patch. Press seams toward the dark fabric.

6. Sew quarter-square triangles on each side of the 5 ¼" rectangles of the remaining 2 Y units. Press seams toward the dark fabric.

7. Sew these Y units to the center block, matching them with their corresponding colored square in the nine-patch. Press seams toward the dark fabric.

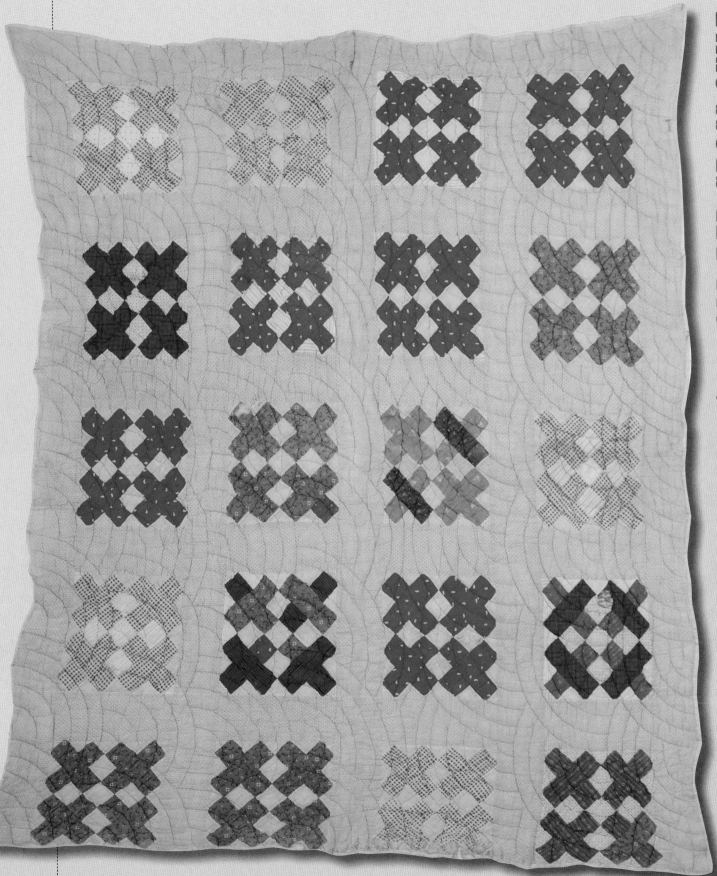

From the collection of Kaye Spitzli

Pattern published by The Kansas City Star, April 5, 1939

Farmer's Fields

FROM GOLDEN'S JOURNAL

"We farmed 80 acres on my folks home place, then the 80 acres south of us which was Amos' grandmother's farm. Then after we moved to the Westerhouse land, my brother Cyril farmed the home place. We had 80 acres of Westerhouse land which was usually in hay. We would make several cuttings of alfalfa a season and sometimes would have neighbors come to help us stack it. We didn't bale it as they do now, but would have 2 or 3 big mounds of stacked hay. I would drive the horses or later the tractor and Amos would pitch it on. After it was on the wagon, he would have to pitch it off onto piles. Later we got the loader which was operated by a rope and pulley.

We also rented Mr. Finley's 160 acres. We had a big wheat acreage over there and sometimes corn. Amos would go there to plant or cultivate and would stay all day so I would pack a meal in boxes to take the children over to the field at noon. There we would try to find some shade to sit under to eat. The "picnic" was fun to begin with, but it got old by the end of the week when the fieldwork was finished."

Amos and Golden working together stacking hay.

Amos Jr., Amos Sr. and possibly "George" (Amos's nickname for Golden) run the binder and tractor, about 1925.

HOW TO MAKE FARMER'S FIELDS

FABRIC REQUIREMENTS

GOLD/GREEN PLAID: 5" x 16"

RED FLOWER PRINT: 5" x 14"

GREEN STRIPE PRINT: 5" x 14"

RED FEATHER PRINT: 5" x 14"

GREEN VINE PRINT: 6" x 16"

FLORAL PRINT W/CREAM BACKGROUND: 2"x 2"

CUTTING INSTRUCTIONS

FROM THE GOLD/GREEN PLAID:

Two 2" squares cut in half diagonally to make a total of 4 half-square A triangles.

In 1940, son Eugene (on tractor) helped Amos in the fields, along with Buck and Topsy.

Two 3 ½" squares cut in half diagonally twice to make a total of 8 quarter-square triangles for B.

FROM THE RED FLOWER PRINT AND THE GREEN STRIPE:

Four 2 ⅛" squares for E.

FROM THE RED FEATHER PRINT:

Four of template D. Mark seam allowance at points (use a ⅛" hole punch on your template to make marking the fabric easier).

FROM THE GREEN VINE PRINT:

Four of template C.
Mark seam allowance at points.

FROM THE FLORAL PRINT WITH CREAM BACKGROUND:

One 1 ½" square for F.

Eugene + the Farmall + Daddy + Buck + Topsy 19--

BLOCK ASSEMBLY

1. Stitch the **shorter side** of piece D onto 1 side of F, starting and stopping ¼" from each edge. Backstitch. Repeat on the opposite side of the center square. Press seams towards the red piece.

2. Stitch the adjoining sides of the trapezoids (shown as black lines on the diagram) beginning at the outside edge, stitch the D sides together ending at the seam of the center square. Backstitch.

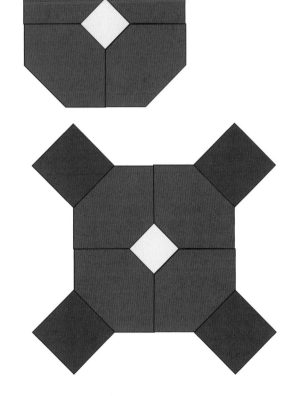

3. Stitch the red flower print E square to the 4 sides of trapezoid D stopping ¼" from the edge. Backstitch.

4. Stitch green vine print trapezoid C along the long sides, beginning and ending ¼" inside seam. Backstitch.

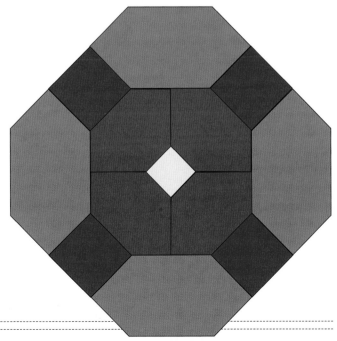

5. Beginning at the outside edge, stitch the short C sides to the red square ending at the seam. Backstitch. Press seams towards red piece.

6. Stitch a gold/green plaid B triangle to 2 sides of the 4 green stripe E squares. Press seams out.

7. Stitch gold/green plaid A triangle to complete the corner.

8. Stitch the 4 corners onto the block. Press.

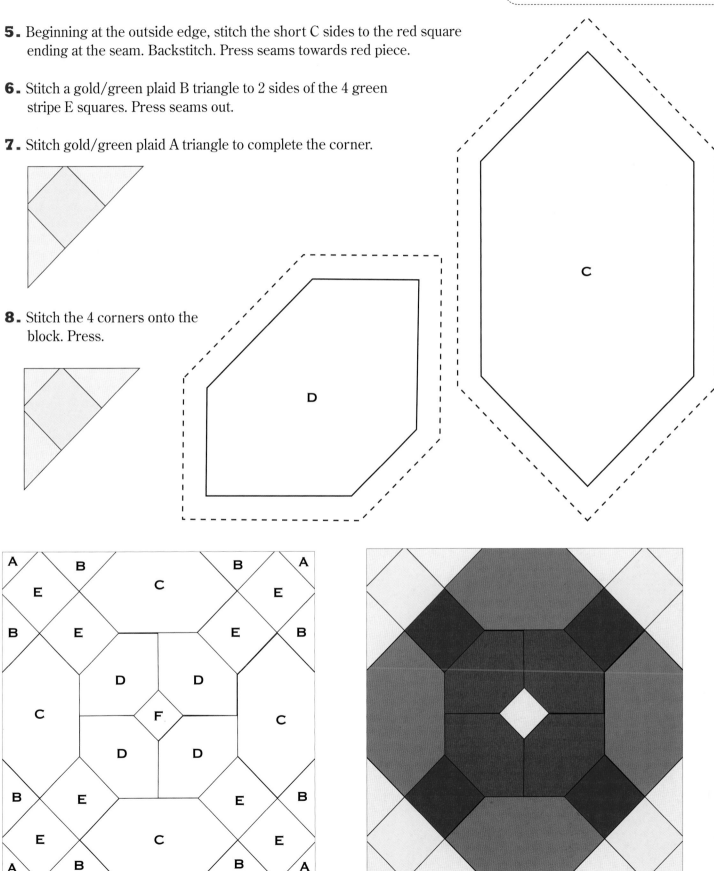

Hens and Chickens

FROM GOLDEN'S JOURNAL

"I have always kept chickens. Sometime in May I would put the brooder hens on their nests to hatch the eggs. By the 4th of July I had fryers to dress. Then in the fall, before winter I would dress the old hens for baking. Early on I just dressed a hen as we needed them, in later years, we could bring the dressed hens to town to the locker plant where we rented freezer space. When we could freeze the hens I would dress 20-25 chickens at a time.

I traded the extra eggs at the Pilla General store and received a token for each dozen eggs. With my tokens we could buy our staples, 100 lbs of flour, 50 lbs. of sugar or even boots and shoes."

Golden feeds the chickens.

Amos, Golden and chicken.

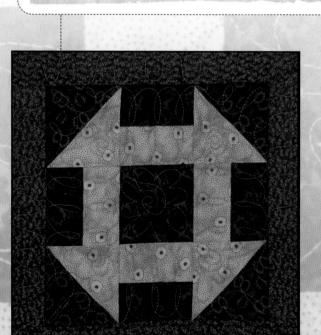

HOW TO MAKE HENS AND CHICKENS

FABRIC REQUIREMENTS

BROWN PRINT: 5" x 10"

RED PRINT: 5" x 14"

TAN PRINT: 5" x 17"

CUTTING INSTRUCTIONS

FROM THE BROWN PRINT:

2 - 3 ⅞" squares cut in half diagonally to make a total of
  4 half-square triangles.

FROM THE TAN PRINT:

2 - 3 ⅞" squares cut in half diagonally to make a total
  of 4 half-square triangles.

4 - 2" x 3 ½" rectangles.

FROM THE RED PRINT:

1 - 3 ½" square.
4 - 2" x 3 ½" rectangles.

BLOCK ASSEMBLY

1. Pair a tan triangle with a brown triangle, right sides together. Sew along the long side. Press the seam toward the brown. Repeat with the remaining triangles. You now have 4 brown/tan squares.

On the back of this photo, Golden wrote: "Me, my chickens and my bathroom."

BLOCK ASSEMBLY CONT.

2. Pair a tan rectangle with a red rectangle, right sides together. Sew along the long side. Press the seam toward the red. Repeat with the remaining rectangles. You now have 4 red/tan squares. Assemble block in rows as shown, press seams, sew rows together.

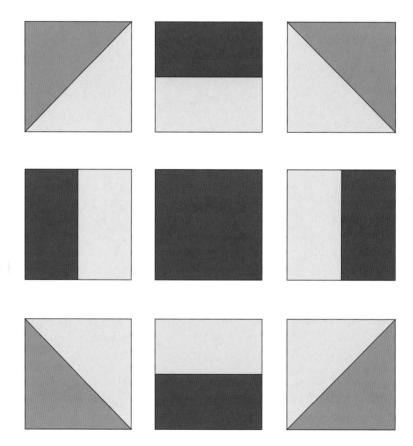

Pattern published by The Kansas City Star. 1939

Pig Pen

FROM GOLDEN'S JOURNAL

"As I raised my hens, Amos always had hogs. He liked raising them - unless they got out, then he would say they always had their heads on the wrong end, as they would never go the direction he wanted them to go. In January when it was real cold, we would butcher two hogs. Amos cut up the bacon slabs and pork roast then take the meat upstairs to the north room for cold storage. We ground our own sausage, then I would fry them in patties and pack them in jars to can. Sunday evening for supper I would make biscuit dough and put the sausage patties inside. In the summer we liked to slice radishes and have leaf lettuce to put with them.

After the good meat was cut up, we would cook all the scraps in the big black iron kettle outside. After it cooled a little, the lard settled on the top and we would fill the lard can. The meat scraps from the bottom would be cooked and canned. I would add this canned scrap meat to mush to make scrapple.

Next we had the fat to cook down into cracklings and lard. I used this for making lye soap for the laundry. After the soap was cooled, and cut into about four inch squares I'd stack it on the back porch by the washer. When I filled the wash tub, I would just put one square of soap into the water. Of course the water to fill the tub would have to be boiled on the wood stove in the kitchen in a copper boiler."

Amos with his hogs.

Written on the back of photo below, taken in 1926: "Daddy was rendering the lard and you know how puppy likes cracklings and how mad it makes him when they feed him a hot one. Well, that's what Daddy just did. Look at those teeth. I wasn't looking to see how much of Daddy I was getting."

HOW TO MAKE PIG PEN

FABRIC REQUIREMENTS

DARK BROWN PRINT: FAT EIGHTH (11" x 18")

LIGHT BROWN PRINT: FAT EIGHTH (11" x 18")

CUTTING INSTRUCTIONS

2 each of templates A, B, and C of the dark print fabric.

2 each of templates A, B, and C of the light print fabric.

BLOCK ASSEMBLY

If you are not experienced in sewing with curves, don't panic:
these are very easy, gentle curves.

1. Beginning with a light print B piece, finger-press to find the center of the
curve. Finger-press a dark print C piece to find the center of the curve,
then place piece B on top of C right sides together, matching the center
markings. Pin at the center and each end.

Tip: You will have less trouble and fewer tucks if you only use 3 pins - don't
be tempted to fill your curve with pins.

2. Keeping piece B on top, stitch, easing the concave (inside) curve to fit
the convex (outside) curve. (Use a stiletto to aid in keeping the edges
together as you stitch.) Press the seam toward the dark print.

BLOCK ASSEMBLY CONT.

3. Finger-press a dark piece A to find the center of the curve. Place right side down on top of the B-C unit, matching centers. Pin at the center and each end. Stitch, then press the seam toward the dark print. Repeat so you have 2 dark, light, dark units.

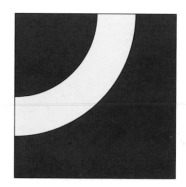

4. Repeat using the light, dark, light combination. Press seam toward the dark print. Repeat so you have 2 light, dark, light units.

5. Stitch units together as shown:

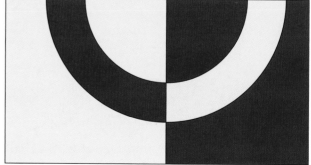

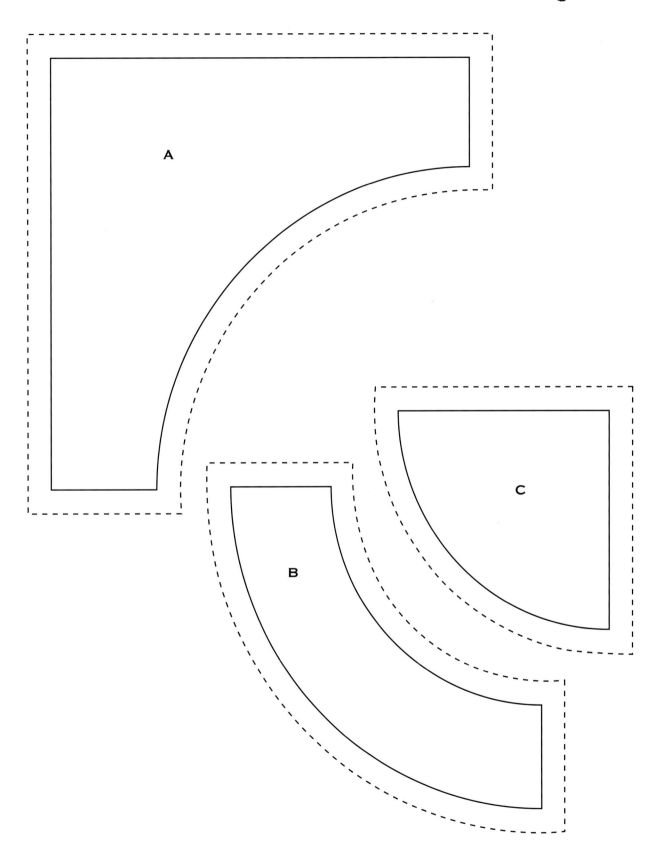

Pattern published by The Kansas City Star, 1935

Farmers Daughter

FROM GOLDEN'S JOURNAL

"Arlene was born on April 28, 1922 while we still lived on the Milburn home place where I was born. A lady friend from Vinland came to stay for a few days until I was able to be up and around. As a youngster, Arlene was always out with Amos and her dog Jack. She would tag along when Amos went to milk and ride the cows out through the lot.

We had moved to the Westerhouse farm before the twins, Eugene and Maxine, were born on August 15, 1927. I was on bed rest for about a month before their birth. My parents moved back to the Milburn home from Kiowa County and my youngest sister, Eva came to stay at our house until after the twins' birth. Eugene had a hernia and every time he'd cry it would raise up. The Doctor was afraid it would rupture. I took Eugene to the hospital in Kansas City for surgery when he was just two weeks old and stayed with him a week or more while he was there.

Golden holds baby Arlene, 1922.

Arlene was in school and Eva kept Maxine. When I finally got home from the hospital with Eugene, Maxine was attached to Eva and didn't want me to hold her.

Amos bought a new Chevrolet soon after they were born. It had side curtains and was really fancy. When the twins were 2 or so they painted the car with used oil!"

Amos and Arlene

Jack and Arlene helping on a wash day, 1924.

HOW TO MAKE FARMER'S DAUGHTER

Note: A rotary cutting version of this block can be found on page 104 (with the Roses for Mama quilt).

FABRIC REQUIREMENTS

BLUE: 6" x 13"

GOLD: 10" x 13"

LIGHT BLUE TOILE: 8" x 11"

CUTTING INSTRUCTIONS

Blue: 8 template A or 8 - 2 ¼" squares.
Gold: 4 each template C and D.
    1 template A.
Light blue toile: 4 template B.

BLOCK ASSEMBLY

1. Mark ¼" seam allowance on all pieces. This can be done easily with a small hole punch. Punch a hole at the beginning and end of each seam on the paper or mylar template. Then place the template over the cut fabric piece and mark a dot through the hole onto the wrong side of fabric.

2. Stitch the 4 C pieces to the D pieces along 1 long side, beginning and ending at the ¼" mark.

C

D

3. Sew 1 blue A square into the end of each joined CD unit. Beginning at the outside edge, stitch to the ¼" mark. Go to the remaining out side edge and stitch to the center ¼" mark.

A

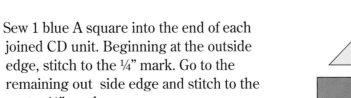

Eugene and Maxine in 1927.

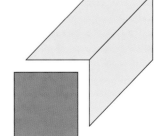

BLOCK ASSEMBLY CONT.

4. Beginning and ending at the ¼" mark, stitch a gold A square between 2 blue A squares.

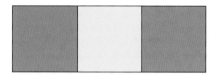

5. Stitch the remaining 2 blue A squares to form the center of the block.

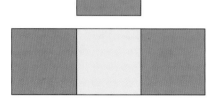

6. Beginning at the outside ¼" mark and ending at the inside ¼" mark, stitch each side of the CD units to the center unit.

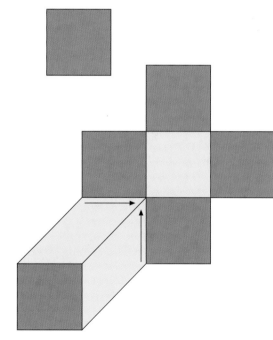

7. Insert the light blue toile B pieces by beginning at the outside edge and stitching to the ¼" mark at the center. Stitch the other side from outside edge to the center. Last, stitch the short seam joining the B piece to the blue A square. Press the seams.

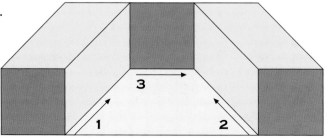

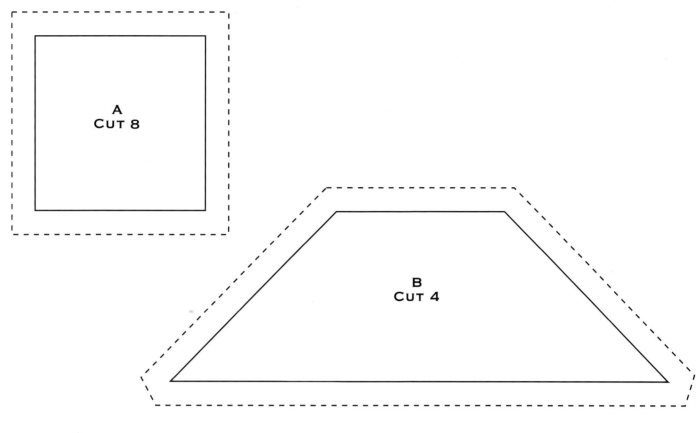

A
CUT 8

B
CUT 4

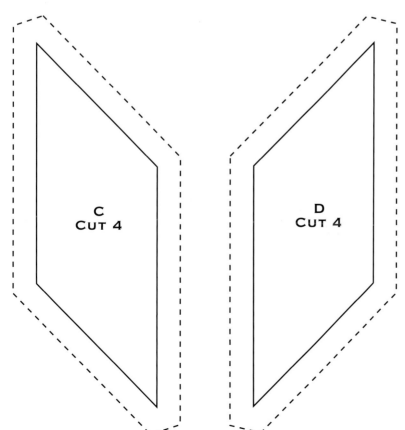

C
CUT 4

D
CUT 4

Pattern published by Mary Elizabeth Johnson 1977

Old Country Church

FROM GOLDEN'S JOURNAL

"We attended Captain Creek Methodist Church, sometimes called 'Little Blue' (because at one time the interior was painted blue). Built in 1884, it was located about a half mile from our home (about a mile from Amos' home place)." One minister served Captain Creek and the Eudora church for many years. Amos and I each attended Sunday School there as children, then as young people to Epworth League. After our children were Sunday School age, we attended regularly. I taught the beginners Sunday School class, was Cradle Roll Superintendent and was the first president of the Women's Society of Christian Service (WSCS) when it was changed from the Women's Missionary Society. Maxine and Gale were married there – the only wedding held in that church. The women all sat on one side and the men on the other until Arlene's suitor, Pete Lawson came one time. He decided he was sitting with her and did. That kind of broke the ice and families began sitting together after that. In 1955 Eudora secured a full time pastor. Captain Creek closed a bit later and we began driving in to Eudora to church."

Captain Creek Church, Hopewell Community

Golden's daughter Maxine Westerhouse and Arvon Gale Gerstenberger were married in the Captain Creek Church June 15, 1948.

HOW TO MAKE OLD COUNTRY CHURCH
FABRIC REQUIREMENTS

BLUE TOILE FOR SKY: **5" x 22"**

GREEN PRINT FOR GRASS: **3 ½" x 12"**

WHITE ON CREAM FOR CHURCH: **5" x 22"**

DARK BLUE FOR DOOR: **2" x 3"**

GOLD PRINT FOR WINDOWS: **2 ½" x 5"**

DARK BROWN PRINT FOR ROOF: **6" x 10"**

ALSO NEEDED: "ADD-A-QUARTER" RULER

PAPER PIECING INSTRUCTIONS

UNIT A

1. Place fabrics for pieces 1 and 2 right sides together and place under the paper, covering section 1 with the wrong side of fabric 1 touching the back of the paper. Make sure the fabric hangs over the line at least ¼" between sections 1 and 2.

2. Sew on the line between sections 1 and 2 using a short stitch length. Stitch a couple of stitches before and after the line.

Press the fabric open.

3. Use an index card (or any card stock) and place the edge of it on the line between pieces 2 and 3.

4. Fold the foundation paper back along the line. (At times, this means tearing paper away from previous stitching.)

5. Using an "Add-a-Quarter" ruler, trim the seam allowance to ¼".

6. Place fabric 3 right sides together with fabric 2, matching the raw edge of piece 3 with the seam allowance you just trimmed on fabric 2.

7. Sew on the line and press the fabric open.

Repeat steps 3-7 for pieces 4 and 5.

Using the "Add-a-Quarter" ruler:

- Trim the seam along the top of pieces 1-5, sew piece 6 and press.

- Trim the seam along the bottom of pieces 1-5, sew piece 7 and press.

- Trim the seam along the left sides of pieces 6, 1, and 7. Sew piece 8 and then press.

- Trim unit A on the dotted line. This will include the seam allowance for the unit.

UNITS B, C, D

Paper piece each unit using the same method as described above.

UNITS E, F, G

Pin paper pattern piece securely to the wrong side of the appropriate fabric and trim along the dotted line.

Old Country Church

PIECING THE UNITS TOGETHER

- Sew unit A to unit D matching the seam that has the "*" in the seam allowance on the pattern.
- Sew unit C to unit A/D matching the seam that has the "$" in the seam allowance on the pattern.
- Sew unit G to one side of the C/A/D unit and unit E to the other side.
- Sew unit B to the top of unit C/A/D and unit F to the bottom of it.
- Carefully tear the paper off the back.

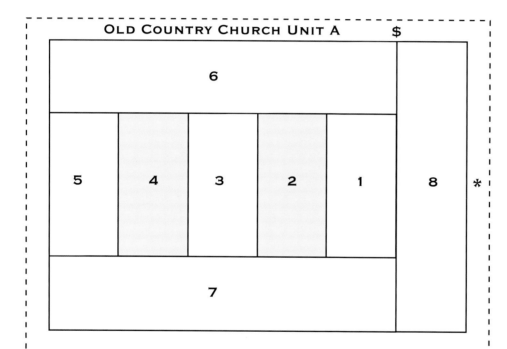

OLD COUNTRY CHURCH UNIT G

OLD COUNTRY CHURCH UNIT A

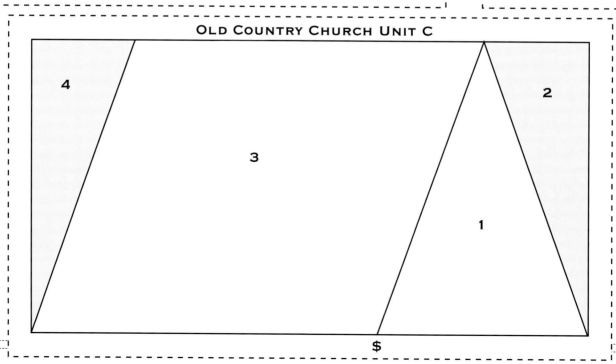

OLD COUNTRY CHURCH UNIT C

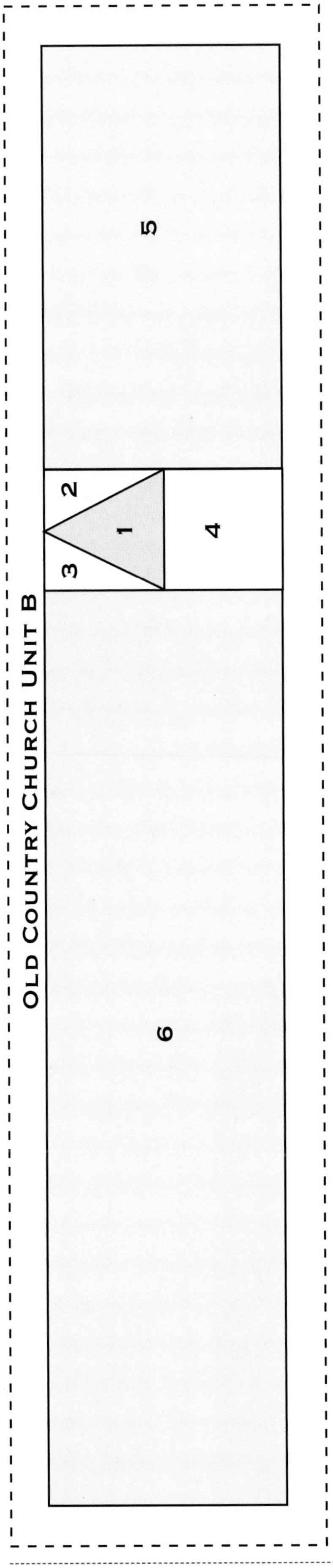

PATTERNS

OLD COUNTRY CHURCH UNIT B

5

2
1
3
4

6

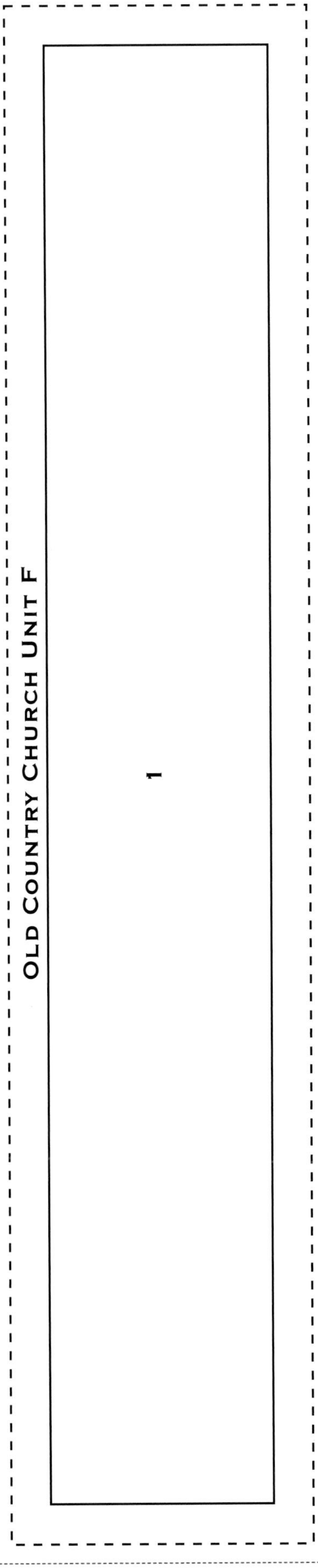

OLD COUNTRY CHURCH UNIT F

1

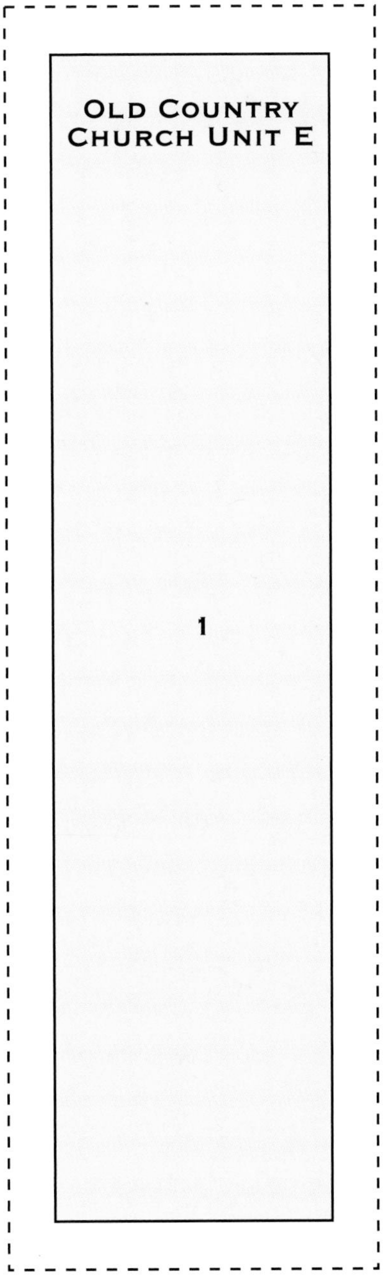

OLD COUNTRY
CHURCH UNIT E

1

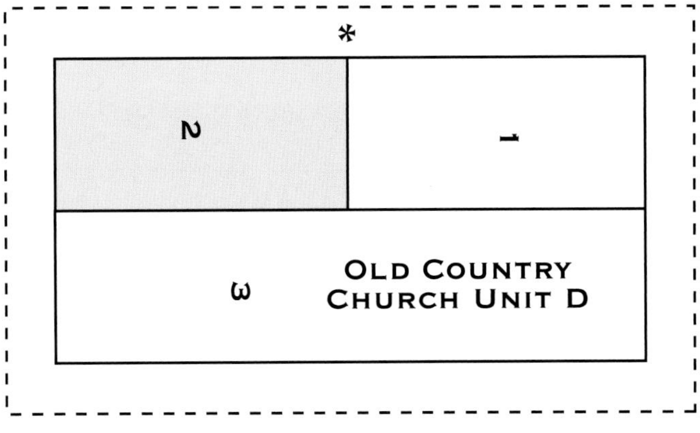

*

2

1

3

OLD COUNTRY
CHURCH UNIT D

Pattern published in The Kansas City Star as French Bouquet, 1931

Grandmother's Flower Garden

FROM GOLDEN'S JOURNAL

"Every spring I planted a big vegetable garden, green beans, potatoes, sweet corn, lettuce, cabbage, onions, radishes, tomatoes, and cucumbers were among the regulars. I liked working in the garden and also enjoyed canning the produce for winter months. We had orchard trees and canned peaches, applesauce, apricots, and cherries. Amos kept several bee hives in the orchard and we enjoyed the honey.

Around the house I had flowers, many perennials and annuals. The old fashioned yellow rose, lilacs, daylilies, iris, zinnias, four-o-clocks, marigolds, phlox, butter and eggs, larkspur and bachelor buttons.

In the fall, we'd plant a fall garden, sweet potatoes, turnips, and more lettuce and spinach."

Daughter Maxine and her lamb in the garden, June 1942.

HOW TO MAKE GRANDMOTHER'S FLOWER GARDEN

FABRIC REQUIREMENTS

WHITE/RED PRINT: 2" SQUARE

LIGHT PINK PRINT: 2" x 12"

PINK PRINT: 2" x 24"

RED PRINT: 2" x 36"

BACKGROUND LIGHT PINK PRINT: 11" x 11"

CUTTING INSTRUCTIONS

1 - 2" square of white/red print for center hexagon.

6 - 2" squares of light pink print for first ring.

12 - 2" squares of pink print for second ring.

18 - 2" squares of red print for outer ring.

BLOCK ASSEMBLY

Use ¾" Mylar* hexagons or cut your own from freezer paper using the template provided.

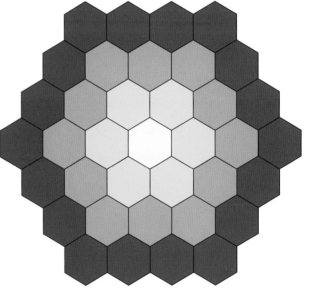

To use Mylar Hexagons:

Place a Mylar hexagon in the center of a 2" square and fold edges over the template. Tack the corners, skipping up to the next corner, or sew a running stitch completely around the inside edges of the hexagon.

Join the hexagon pieces together with a whip stitch. Start with the first ring around the center hexagon, whip stitch the base of each light pink hexagon to the center hexagon then whip stitch the sides of the light pink hexagons to each other. Add the next ring, sewing only the base of the hexagons. Remove Mylar from the first ring and sew the sides of the hexagons. Add the next rings in the same manner. Leave the pieces of Mylar in the outer ring until it has been appliquéd onto the background. Cut out the background fabric from behind.

Golden hoeing in her garden.

Grandmother's Flower Garden

BLOCK ASSEMBLY

TO USE FREEZER PAPER TEMPLATES:

Copy the template pattern (not including seam allowance) onto freezer paper. (*Hint:* Stack several sheets of paper together, staple, then cut out several template papers at once.) Iron freezer paper hexagon onto the back side of fabric. Cut out hexagon, leaving a ¼" seam allowance around the paper pattern. Fold the seam allowance to the back and baste through the freezer paper. Stitch hexagons together as directed above, however, leave all paper in until after it has been appliquéd onto the background.

Center the finished hexagon "flower" onto the background fabric and appliqué around the block.

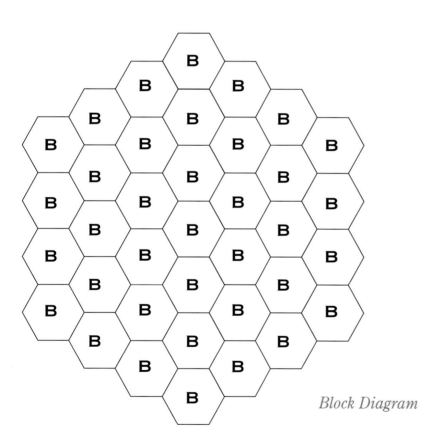

Block Diagram

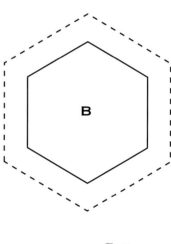

Pattern

Pattern published by Hinson, 1966

Schoolhouse

FROM GOLDEN'S JOURNAL

"Our children, Arlene, Eugene and Maxine also attended Hopewell School through the eighth grade.

We had an old dog named Bingo who would wander up to meet them each afternoon for the walk home. One Friday evening Bingo was missing and the children called and called for him and all day Saturday. Sunday morning we were on our way to church and as we passed the schoolhouse we could hear Bingo barking. The children began crying "There's Bingo!" and sure enough, there was Bingo...he had gotten locked inside the school spent his weekend chewing his way through the big oak front door! So here he was with his head poked out the hole in the front door. The children were delighted to have their dog back, but Amos was slightly less delighted to spend his Sunday afternoon replacing the door of the schoolhouse."

Above: Eugene and Maxine, ready for school.
Below: Arlene with her lunch pail and the twins.

HOW TO MAKE SCHOOLHOUSE
FABRIC REQUIREMENTS

BACKGROUND PRINT: 12" x 22"

BROWN PRINT: 12" x 22"

BLOCK ASSEMBLY

PAPER PIECING INSTRUCTIONS

(Pattern sheets with numbered pieces)
Note: There are 7 different units that make up the schoolhouse block. Begin with Unit A.

UNIT A

Place fabrics for pieces 1 and 2 right sides together and place under the paper covering section 1 with the wrong side of fabric 1 touching the back of the paper. Make sure the fabric hangs over the line between sections 1 and 2 at least ¼".

Sew on the line between sections 1 and 2 using a short stitch length. Stitch a couple of stitches before and after the line. Press the fabric open.

Using an index card (or any card stock), and place the edge of it on the line between pieces 2 and 3. Fold the foundation paper back along the line. (At times,

this means tearing paper away from previous stitching.)

Using an "Add-a-Quarter" ruler, (see Resources, page 127) trim the seam to ¼" then line up and sew piece 3 to piece 2 right sides together.

Continue this process, adding each piece in numerical order until you have completed a unit. Repeat this process for remaining units.

Trim each unit on the dotted lines. This will include the seam allowance for the unit.

SCHOOLHOUSE UNIT A

8

7

1   2   3

5   6   9

4

PIECE THE UNITS TOGETHER:

Refer to the block photo to assemble the units.

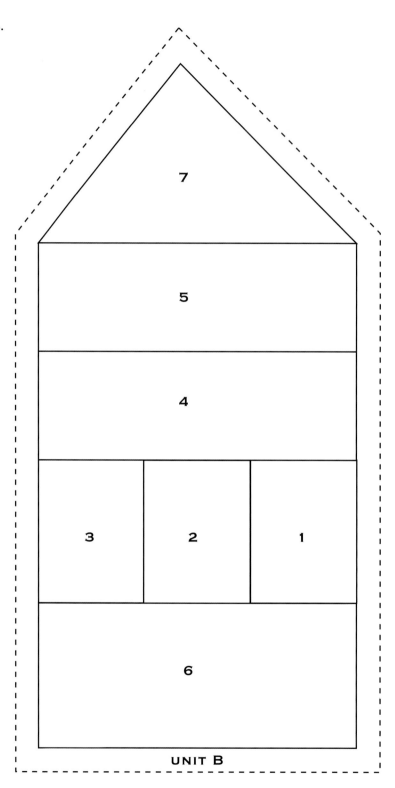

7

5

4

3   2   1

6

UNIT B

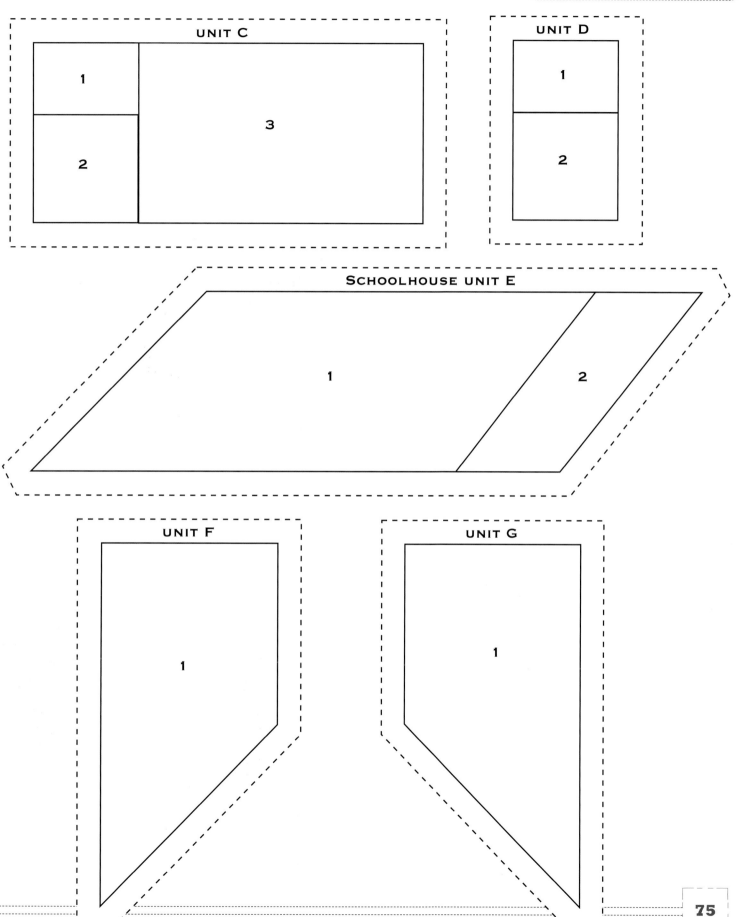

Sunflower

FROM GOLDEN'S JOURNAL

Pattern published by Old Chelsea Station, a mail-order company begun in 1933. The block was credited to Carol Curtis.

"Fall harvest was always a busy time. The men worked until late in the fields and we women were busy gathering in the remainder of the garden produce, canning, cooking big meals for the harvest help and often helping in the fields ourselves.

Gathering walnuts from the timber was always a fall Sunday afternoon event. The walnuts would then be dumped out in the drive way where we drove over them until the husks broke away. Then they were bagged up and stored in the barn until Amos cracked a few and brought some to the house. During long winter evenings we would sit at the table by the stove and pick out the walnut meats."

Amos in foreground on the wagon with corn and pumpkins.

HOW TO MAKE SUNFLOWER

FABRIC REQUIREMENTS

GREEN FLORAL BACKGROUND: 10" x 10"

TAN FLORAL CORNERS: 3 ½" x 11"

TWO RED PRINTS FOR PETALS: 4" x 8" EACH

TWO GOLD PRINTS FOR PETALS: 4" x 8" EACH

GREEN PLAID FOR CENTER: 4" x 4"

CUTTING INSTRUCTIONS

Green floral background: 9 ½" square.

Tan floral (corners): 4 - 2 3/8" squares.

Two gold w/red prints (petals): 3 each of template C.

Two red prints (petals): 3 each of template C.

Green plaid (flower center): 1 of template D.**

**Tip: Cut circle D using pinking sheers to ease the bulk of the curve.*

BLOCK ASSEMBLY

1. Draw a diagonal line on the wrong side of the 4 - 2 ³⁄₈" tan floral squares. Place 1 tan square on each corner of the background right sides together so the line does not run to the corner of the block. Stitch on the diagonal line.

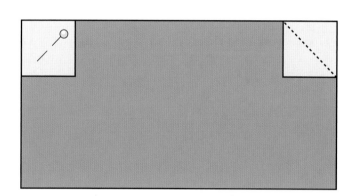

2. Trim ¼" from the seam on the side closest to the corner. Press toward triangle.

The entire family gathered walnuts.

BLOCK ASSEMBLY CONT.

3. Make a small hole on both sides of template C (where the "roof" meets the "sides"). Mark a dot in the wrong side of each fabric petal at the seam line through this hole.

4. Lay out the petals to form the sunflower alternating the 4 prints. You will have 3 groups of the 4 fabrics to make a complete ring of petals.

5. Sew petals right sides together from the center to the marked dot, backstitching at the dot to form the petal ring. Press seams open.

6. Using heat resistant plastic or light weight cardstock, make a template C **without** the ¼" seam allowance. Lay this template on the wrong side of each petal of the petal ring and press the seam allowance of the petal points over the template to form sharp perfect petal points.

7. Fold the background square into quarters and press creases to mark the center of the block for placement. Fold the petal ring into quarters and pin or glue baste onto the center of the background. Appliqué the outside edges of the petal ring onto the background square.

8. Using heat resistant plastic or light weight cardstock, make a template D **without** the ¼" seam allowance. Lay this template on the wrong side of the fabric circle and press the seam allowance over the template to form a perfect circle.

9. Appliqué the fabric circle to the center of the sunflower. Place the block face down on the ironing board and press.

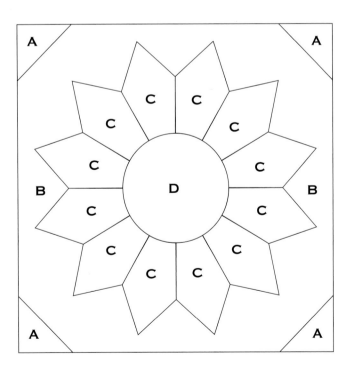

Block Diagram

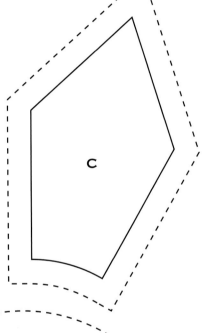

Pattern published by The Kansas City Star. 1947

Snowball

FROM GOLDEN'S JOURNAL

"When the weather turned cold we closed off the kitchen as everything froze out there even with the wood cook stove going. There was big heating stove in the dining room that held a great big chunk of wood. We could close off the rest of the house and the whole family even slept on the floor there during the winter.

Amos would go out for chores but come in, strip off all his wet clothes which then would be laid out to dry in front of the stove. The children loved those cold days as he would stay in during the daytime playing games and cards with them. Sometimes he would hitch the sled behind the horse for snow rides. I gathered eggs at least three times a day to keep them from freezing. Any farm animals that arrived early had to be brought into the house. Many times we had baby pigs penned up back behind the stove.

A heavy snowfall in 1936 closed the roads for several days.

When we could get out we would go to church in the spring wagon. Amos put straw in the bottom and I would take old blankets and comforts to cover up the children. Amos and I would ride up on the seat with the kids down in the straw under blankets. The harnesses we used had jingle bells and during church we could hear the horses jingling and stamping while they waited on us.

The children normally walked to school in the snow through grade school but then during Arlene's high school years (1936-1940) we had terrible snows. She stayed in town with Grandpa Westerhouse. Amos would go in for supplies on Friday and bring her home for the weekends during her freshman year. Later she was able to ride to town and back home with a neighbor, Gus Gabriel who managed the elevator in town. Pete Lawson was a farm hand at a nearby farm and also rode into town with the Mr. Gabriel. They became sweethearts and then married in 1942.

Sometimes Amos would walk ahead of the children, making a path for them to walk in."

Getting off the high school bus on another snowy day.

HOW TO MAKE SNOWBALL
Fabric Requirements

Large floral print: **7" x 12"**

Neutral w/green print: **3 ½" x width of fabric**

Green print: **3 ½" x width of fabric**

Red print: **3 ½" x 20"**

CUTTING INSTRUCTIONS

FROM THE LARGE FLORAL PRINT:

2 - 5" squares.

FROM THE NEUTRAL WITH GREEN PRINT:

2 - 2" x 9" strips.
1 - 2" x 6" strip.

FROM THE GREEN PRINT:

1 - 2" x 9" strip.
2 - 2" x 6" strip.

FROM THE RED PRINT:

8 - 2" squares.

BLOCK ASSEMBLY

FOR THE NINE PATCHES:

Sew 2 - 9" strip sets, placing the green print strip in between 2 neutral w/green print strips. Press the seams toward the green center strip.

Sew 1- 6" strip set placing the neutral w/green print strip in between 2 green print strips. Press seams toward the outside green strips.

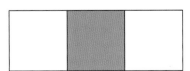

Sub-cut the 9" strip sets into 4 - 2" strips.

BLOCK ASSEMBLY CONT.

Sub-cut the 6" strip set into 2 - 2" strips.

Assemble the 2 nine-patch sections as shown:

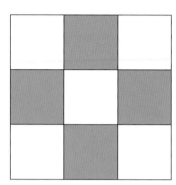

FOR THE SNOWBALL SQUARES:

Draw a diagonal line on the back side of the 8 red print 2" squares.

Place these squares in each corner of the 2 - 5" large floral print squares, right sides together. Stitch along the diagonal line. Trim off the corner leaving a ¼" seam allowance. Press the seam open.

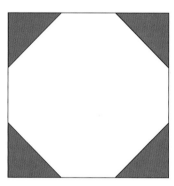

Make 2

Stitch together as shown:

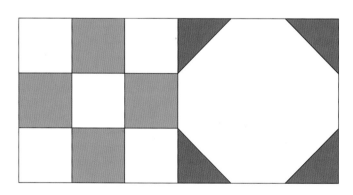

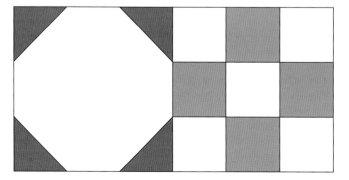

By Kaye Spitzli, quilted by Eula Lang 2006

Tree of Life

FROM GOLDEN'S JOURNAL

"We often hosted family dinners. Whenever mother's sister Ida came, we would all get together for the day. Ida's husband was a minister and all the children loved him so. They would gather around him and he'd tell stories, which he made up as he talked.

We often had as many as 35 or 40 people. Aunt Ida's of course would be staying overnight and be there for breakfast, the others would just come for the day. I would dress chickens and make pies. Tables extended through the living room and dining room and also in the kitchen. During the summer the children would be outside at a table. Afterwards we would sit and visit until the dishes were dry and had to soak before they would wash easily.

After dinner, the children played hide and seek all over the farm while the grown-ups visited. The men often froze ice cream in the afternoon. They would sit around the windmill and visit while taking turns at the crank. By five o'clock it was chore time and most would head home to do chores."

A visit from Uncle Frank and Aunt Ida's family was always cause for a celebration.

A Milburn family gathering.

HOW TO MAKE TREE OF LIFE

FABRIC REQUIREMENTS

NEUTRAL BACKGROUND PRINT: **8" x 20"**

BROWN PRINT: **4" x 6"**

RED LARGE FLORAL PRINT: **8" x 11"**

GREEN PRINT: **4" x 9"**

PURPLE PRINT: **4" x 6"**

GOLD PRINT: **4" x 6"**

CUTTING INSTRUCTIONS

FROM BACKGROUND FABRIC:

1 - 5 ¾" square. Cut twice diagonally to make 4 quarter-square triangles. (You will only use 2 of these triangles.)

9 - 2 ⅜" squares. Cut once diagonally to make 18 half-square triangles.

2 - 2" squares.

FROM THE RED LARGE PRINT:

1 - 6 ⅞" square. Cut once diagonally to make 2 half-square triangles. (You will only use 1 of these triangles.)

2 - 2 ⅜" squares.

FROM THE PURPLE PRINT:

2 - 2 ⅜" squares. Cut once diagonally to make 4 half-square triangles.

FROM THE GOLD PRINT:

2 - 2 ⅜" squares. Cut once diagonally to make 4 half-square triangles.

FROM THE GREEN PRINT:

3 - 2 ⅜" squares. Cut once diagonally to make 6 half-square triangles.

FOR BROWN TREE TRUNK:

1 - 2 ⅝" x 5" rectangle.

Tree of Life

BLOCK ASSEMBLY

1. Sew 1 of the background quarter-square triangles to each side of the brown trunk strip as shown.

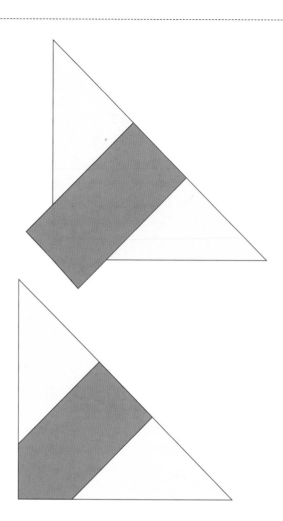

2. Place a square ruler over this unit and trim the tree trunk.

3. Stitch 1 large red floral half-square triangle to form the tree.

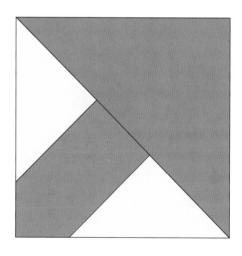

4. Pair a background 2 ⅜" triangle with a print 2 ⅜" triangle, right sides together. Sew along the long side. Press the seam toward the print. Repeat with the remaining 17 sets of triangles. Make 18 square units. Press open, pressing the seam towards the colored print.

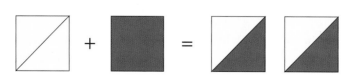

5. Stitch 8 of the half-square triangles into 2 rows of 4 as shown. Press the seams of row 1 all up and the seams of row 2 all down.

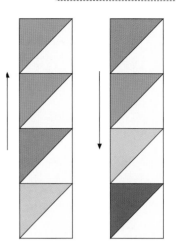

6. Stitch together the 2 rows, butting the seams so the points meet. Press the seam.

7. Stitch this unit to the tree unit as shown. Press seams toward the tree.

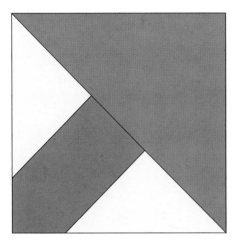
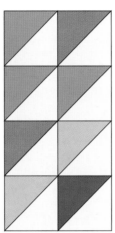

8. Stitch the remaining half-square triangles and 2" squares into rows as shown. Press the seams of row 1 all to the left and the seams of row 2 all to the right. (Note the angle change on the last half-square triangle of the second row.)

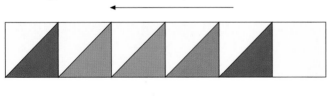

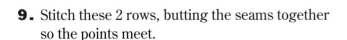

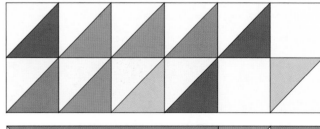

9. Stitch these 2 rows, butting the seams together so the points meet.

10. Stitch this unit to the tree as shown. Press seams.

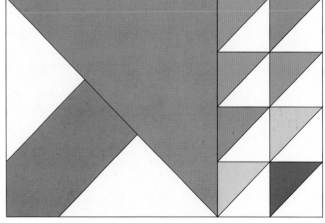

Basket

FROM GOLDEN'S JOURNAL

"Golden's basket was used regularly - to deliver eggs to customers or to carry pies and fried chicken to church dinners. Our lives are like baskets, they hold memories, stories and treasures to be shared. It is our hope that these blocks have caused you to remember your family stories. Inside your basket, you may want to place your name, date, and any other information needed to pass on to the future generations the stories of faith, family, and needlework."

In the book of Joshua, chapter 4, as the Israelites were about to cross the Jordan River, God instructed them to carry twelve stones from the middle of the river and pile them up at the place where they camped that night. These stones were used as a memorial - when your children ask, "What do these stones mean...then you can tell them…"

Golden's basket on one of her many quilts.

HOW TO MAKE BASKET

FABRIC REQUIREMENTS

BACKGROUND FABRIC: 11" x 22"

BROWN PRINT: FAT QUARTER (18" x 22")

PINK PRINT: 3" x 22"

CUTTING INSTRUCTIONS

FROM BACKGROUND FABRIC:

1 - 9 ⅞" square. Cut this diagonally to make 2 half-square triangles. (You will only use 1 of these triangles.)

2 - 1 ⅝" x 7 ⅝" rectangles.

1 - 3 ⅛" square.

FROM THE PINK PRINT:

7 - 2" squares then cut once diagonally to make 14 half-square triangles.

1 - 1 ⅝" square.

FROM THE BROWN PRINT:

7 - 2" squares then cut once diagonally to make 14 half-square triangles.

6 - 1 ⅝" squares.

1 - 3 ⅛" square

1 - 1 ½" x 14" bias strip.

BLOCK ASSEMBLY

1. Pair a brown 2" triangle with a pink 2" triangle, right sides together. Sew along the long side. Press the seam toward the brown. Repeat with the remaining 13 sets of triangles. Makes 14 half-square units.

2. Draw a diagonal line on the wrong side of the 3 ⅛" background square. Place it right sides together on the 3 ⅛" brown square. Stitch **directly on the diagonal line**. Trim ¼" from stitched seam. Press open. Trim to 2 ⅝" square.

3. Draw a diagonal line on the wrong side of the 1 ⅝" pink print square. Place right side down over the brown section of the 2 ⅝" half-square triangle just completed. Stitch on the **diagonal line**. Trim ¼" from stitched seam. Press open. Trim to 2 ⅝" square.

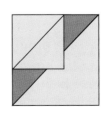 

BLOCK ASSEMBLY CONT.

4. Sew together 4 half-square units and one 1 ⅝" brown square into a strip. Press seams.

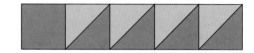

5. Sew this strip to 1 - 1 ⅝" x 7 ⅝" background rectangle, allowing the extra rectangle fabric to extend to the left of the brown print square. Press seam.

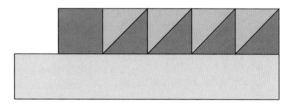

6. Sew the 2 ⅝" square from Step 3 to the right side of this strip. Press seam.

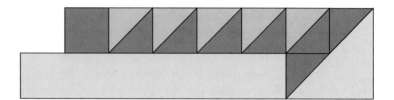

7. Sew together 4 half-square units and 1 - 1 ⅝" brown square into a strip. Press seams.

Sew together 3 half-square units and 1 - 1 ⅝" brown square into a strip. Press seams.

Sew together 2 half-square units and 1 - 1 ⅝" brown square into a strip. Press seams.

Sew together 1 half-square units and 1 - 1 ⅝" brown square into a strip. Press seams.

Sew together all the strips so that the half-square units form a straight edge and the brown squares look like a staircase descending. Sew the remaining 1 ⅝" brown square to this unit to finish the stair steps. Press seams.

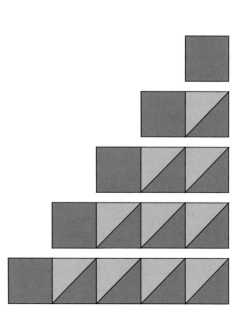

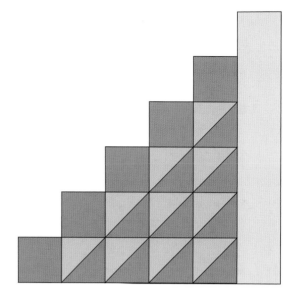

8. Stitch the remaining 1 ⅝" x 7 ⅝" background strip to the right side of this unit. Press seams.

9. Stitch the unit from Step 6 to the unit from Step 8. Press seams.

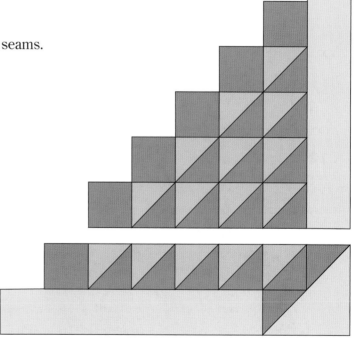

*Eula quilted a flower in this basket block
made of 1930s reproductions.*

BLOCK ASSEMBLY CONT.

10. Draw a gentle arc on the large background triangle. (Use a small plate then just trace the top arc.) Be sure you are at least ¾" from the edge. Fold the 14" bias strip wrong sides together, press. Place the folded bias over the drawn line with the raw edges towards the top point of the triangle. Stitch a ¼" seam from the raw edge. Trim the seam. Press the folded edge up over the seam and hand stitch down.

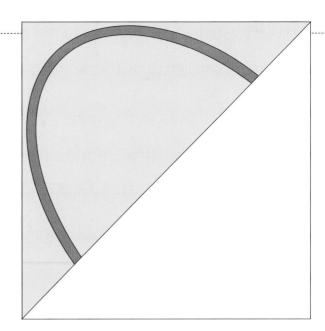

11. Lay the handle unit from Step 10 on top of the basket unit from Step 9, right sides together. Keep the top point of the handle triangle even with the bottom point of the basket triangle. The stair step edges of the 1 ⅝" brown squares will stick out from the bias edges of the triangles. Stitch, using a ¼" seam allowance. Trim to even the edges. Press open.

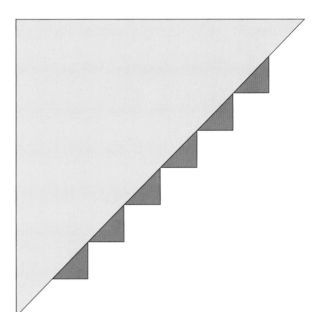

12. Using an archival pen, or hand or machine embroidery, sign and date your quilt block.

Projects and Settings

Hugs and Kisses

Hugs and Kisses Tablerunner, 15" x 33"
Made by Arlene Lawson, Golden's daughter

FABRIC REQUIREMENTS

WHITE WITH RED PRINT: $^3/_8$ YARD

5 RED WITH WHITE PRINTS:

    FOR BORDER AND BINDING: $^5/_8$ YARD

    FOR PIG PEN BLOCK AND 1 CROSS IN EACH BLOCK: $^1/_4$ YARD

    FOR THE OTHER 3 CROSSES IN EACH BLOCK: $^1/_8$ YARD OF EACH OF 3 REDS

CUTTING INSTRUCTIONS

For the Pig Pen block, see page 56.
For the Red Cross block, see page 44.
Border: 2 - 3 ½" x 27 ½"
        2 - 3 ½" x 15 ½"
Binding: 3 - 2 ½" x width of fabric strips

QUILT ASSEMBLY

1. Following the instructions on page 57, assemble 1 Pig Pen block using the white with red print and 1 red with white print.

2. Following the instructions on page 45, assemble 2 Red Cross blocks using the white with red print as the background and 4 red with white prints for the 4 crosses in each block. Make each cross out of a different fabric.

3. Sew the 3 blocks into a row, with the Pig Pen block between the 2 Red Cross blocks.

4. Sew the 2 ½" x 27 ½" strips to both long sides of the block strips.

5. Sew the 2 ½" x 15 ½" strips to both short sides of the block strips.

6. Quilt your tablerunner as desired.

7. Bind, using the 2 ½" strips.

Golden Wedding Day

FABRIC REQUIREMENTS

Refer to the letters assigned to each color for placement in the blocks.

MEDIUM LAVENDER (COLOR A):
 ⅓ YARD
BLUE (COLOR B): ¼ YARD
PURPLE (COLOR C): ⅓ YARD
LAVENDER PRINT (COLOR D): ⅔ YARD
LIGHT LAVENDER (COLOR E): ¼ YARD

CUTTING INSTRUCTIONS

MEDIUM LAVENDER (A):

2 - 1 ½" x 7"
9 - 1 ½" x 13"

BLUE (B):

2 - 1 ½" x 7"
5 - 1 ½" x 13"

PURPLE (C):

2 - 1 ½" x 7"
7 - 1 ½" x 13"
2 - 1" x 18 ½"
2 - 1" x 19 ½"

LAVENDER PRINT (D):

2 - 1 ½" x 7"
9 - 1 ½" x 13"
2 - 2 ½" x 19 ½"
2 - 2 ½" x 23 ½"
3 - 2" x width of fabric for binding

LIGHT LAVENDER (E):

1 - 1 ½" x 7"
6 - 1 ½" x 13"

BLOCK ASSEMBLY

1. Sew the 7" strips in color order for Row 5, cut these strips crosswise to make 4 - 1 ½" row units.

2. In the same manner, sew the 13" strips in order for Rows 1+9, 2+8, 3+7, 4+6. Cut these strips crosswise to make 8 - 1 ½" row units from each.

Row 1+9: A, C, E, D, A, D, E, C, A

Row 2+8: C, E, D, A, B, A, D, E, C

Row 3+7: E, D, A, B, C, B, A, D, E

Row 4+6: D, A, B, C, D, C, B, A, D

Row 5: A, B, C, D, E, D, C, B, A

3. Lay out the units in order and press the seams in alternate directions.

GOLDEN WEDDING DAY   23" x 23"   *Made and quilted by Nan Doljac*

Golden Wedding Day

BLOCK ASSEMBLY

3. Lay out the units in order and press the seams in alternate directions.

4. Sew together rows to make 4 blocks.

5. Sew the 4 blocks together.

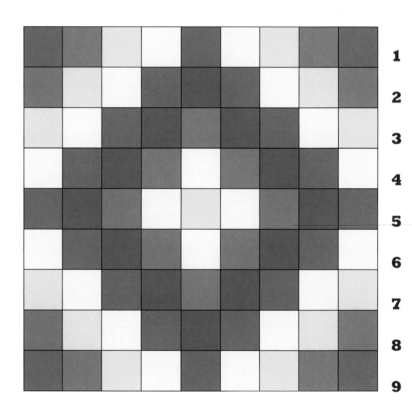

1
2
3
4
5
6
7
8
9

BORDERS

6. Sew a 1" x 18 ½" purple strip to the 2 sides.

7. Sew a 1" x 19 ½" purple strip to the top and bottom.

8. Sew a 2 ½" x 19 ½" lavender print strip to the 2 sides.

9. Sew a 2 ½" x 23 ½" lavender print strip to the top and bottom.

10. Quilt, bind with the 2" lavender print strips.

The Milburn family home, where Golden grew up. She and Amos lived there in the early years of their marriage.

Cabin Windows

FABRIC REQUIREMENTS

BLUE FOR BLOCKS AND SASHING: 1 YARD

RED FOR BLOCKS AND BORDER FLANGE: 1 ¼ YARD

CREAM FOR BLOCKS: 1 ¾ YARD

DARK BLUE FOR SASHING AND BINDING: ⅝ YARD

BLUE FOR INNER BORDER: ⅗ YARD

BLUE PRINT FOR OUTER BORDER: 1 YARD

BACKING: 3 ⅓ YARDS

REFER TO THE BLOCK ON PAGE 18 FOR CUTTING AND ASSEMBLY INSTRUCTIONS.

Make 4 blocks of this color variation.

Make 5 blocks of this color variation.

Make 4 blocks of this color variation.

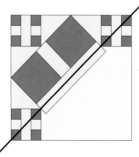

Make 8 blocks in this color variation. They will be trimmed on the diagonal once they are sewn into the quilt, to make the side setting triangles.

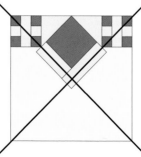

Make 4 of this color variation. These will be the corner setting triangles when trimmed diagonally through both corners.

CABIN WINDOWS   49" x 49"   *Made by Reeze Hanson*

Cabin Windows

SASHING AND TOP ASSEMBLY

1. Mark the side setting triangles and corner triangles on the stitching line (directly through the diagonal). Trim each of these units ¼" from the marked stitching line.

2. Arrange blocks and setting triangles on a design wall to ensure correct placement of each color variation, using the photo on page 101 as a guide.

3. Cut 18 strips of blue sashing fabric 1" x 9 ½". Place these between blocks in a row and sew rows together as shown.

4. Cut 1 – 9 ½" x 20" strip of blue fabric. Cut 1 – 1" x 20" strip of dark blue fabric. Stitch the dark blue narrow strip to the top of the light blue wide strip. Press toward the wide strip. Subcut this strip set into 18 – 1" slices. Stitch together end to end to make the sashing between the rows. Make 2 rows of 3 strips, 2 rows of 5 strips, and 2 rows of 1 strip.

5. Join sashing rows to block rows, carefully matching seam lines. Press toward the sashing.

BORDERS

INNER BORDER
Cut 4 – 1 ½" x width of fabric (wof) blue strips.

FLANGE
Cut 4 – 1" x wof red strips.

A flange is a lengthwise folded strip of fabric inserted between the right sides of 2 borders of a quilt. The raw edges of all pieces are lined up, then stitched through all layers. The flange will appear like a small border and can add a splash of color— without sewing in another border.

OUTER BORDER
Cut 4 – 4" x wof red and blue print strips.

CORNER BLOCKS
Cut 4 - 4" cream squares.

1. Measure length of quilt through the center and cut 2 inner border strips to this measurement. Stitch to the sides of the quilt top. Press seam allowance toward the border. Measure the width of the top through the center, and cut 2 inner border strips to this measurement, and stitch to the top and bottom of the quilt top, pressing toward the border.

2. Fold the red tonal flange in half lengthwise and press carefully. Cut off any selvages. Align the raw edges of the flange with the outer edge of the inner border. Baste these strips to all 4 sides of the quilt top using a ⅛" seam and a long basting stitch. Allow the flange strips to overlap one another at the corners.

3. Measure the width and height of the quilt cut the 4 outer border strips to this measurement. Sew the side borders on the first and press seam allowance toward the border. Then sew the corner blocks to both ends of the top and bottom border strips, pressing seam allowance away from the corner block. Sew in place, matching seam lines. Press seam allowance toward the border.

Flour Sack Tea Towel

Made by Christina DeArmond

MATERIALS NEEDED

FLOUR SACK TOWEL

BROWN .05 PIGMA PEN

EMBROIDERY FLOSS IN YOUR CHOICE OF COLORS

STITCHING INSTRUCTIONS

1. Trace 3 flowers plus the leaves and vine that go with them (use the flower embroidery pattern on page 117) onto a flour sack tea towel, using a Pigma pen. Center the middle flower on the bottom middle edge of the towel.

2. Using 3 strands of embroidery floss, embroider the traced shapes using a stem stitch (see Stem Stitch on page 11).

3. Use the same color for each flower or make them all different colors.

4. *Optional:* Fill in the flower centers with French knots (see French Knots on page 11).

Roses for Mama Quilt

FABRIC REQUIREMENTS

Note: This quilt setting gives a rotary-cut version of the Farmer's Daughter block shown using templates on page 61. The rotary cut block finishes at 8 ½" rather than 9" like the rest of the sampler blocks.

FLOWER PRINT: 2 ⅛ YARDS

PINK: 1 ¾ YARDS

GREEN: 1 YARD

CREAM PRINT: ½ YARD

BORDER STRIPE: 2 ⅞ YARDS

CUTTING INSTRUCTIONS

FROM THE FLOWER PRINT:

17 – 9" squares for Snowball blocks

FROM THE PINK:

72 – 2 ⅝" squares cut in half diagonally once (144 triangles)

140 – 2 ¼" squares for Snowball block and border stripe strip corners

FROM THE GREEN:

7 – 1" x width of the fabric (wof) strips for inner border

72 – 2 ⅝" squares cut in half diagonally once (144 triangles)

72 – 2 ¼" squares for border stripe strip corners

FROM THE CREAM PRINT:

72 – 2 ¼" squares for nine-patch blocks

FROM THE BORDER STRIPE:

2 – 5" x 80" length of fabric (lof) strips for outer border sides

2 – 5" x 60" lof strips for outer border top and bottom

4 – 2 ½" x 80" lof strips for binding

90 – 2 ¼" squares fussy cut (centering the flowers) in the nine-patches and block frames

72 – 2 ¼" x 5 ⅞" strips border for the Farmer's Daughter block frame

BLOCK ASSEMBLY

SNOWBALL BLOCKS

1. Using the 9" squares of flower print and 68 of the pink 2 ¼" squares, sew 17 Snowball blocks following the instructions on page 81.

ROSES FOR MAMA   56" x 74"   *Made by Kaye Spitzli, quilted by Eula Lang*

Roses for Mama

BLOCK ASSEMBLY

FARMER'S DAUGHTER BLOCKS

1. Sew a green half-square triangle to a pink half-square triangle to make a green/pink 2 ¼" square. Repeat until you have made 72.

2. Sew 17 nine-patch blocks using 4 green/pink squares, 4 cream print squares and 1 fussy cut flower square.

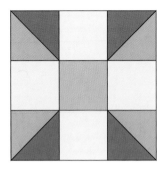

3. Sew 72 green squares to each side of 36 – 2 ¼" x 5 ⅞" strips using the Snowball corner method.

4. Sew 72 pink squares to each side of 36 – 2 ¼" x 5 ⅞" strips using the Snowball corner method.

5. Sew 1 fussy cut flower 2 ¼" square to each end of each frame strip with green half-square triangles (72 strips).

6. Sew 1 frame strip with pink half-square triangles to both sides of each nine-patch.

7. Sew 1 green/frame strip unit to the top and bottom of this unit.

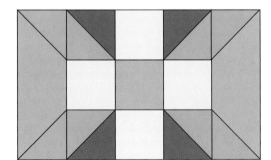

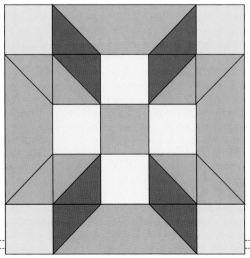

QUILT ASSEMBLY

1. Sew 2 Snowball blocks between 3 Farmer's Daughter blocks (Row A). Make 4 A rows.

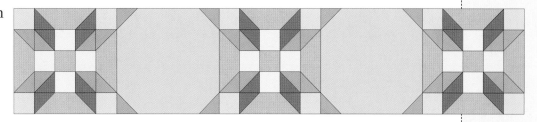

2. Sew 2 Farmer's Daughter blocks between 3 Snowball blocks (Row B). Make 3 B rows.

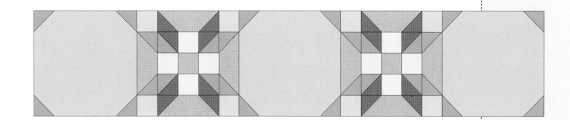

3. Sew strips together in this order: Row A, B, A, B, A, B and ending with row A.

4. Sew 1" green inner border to sides.

5. Sew green inner border to top and bottom.

6. Beginning and ending with backstitching ¼" inside the raw edge, sew the outside border strips to each side of the quilt, leaving an 8" overhang on each end.

7. Beginning and ending with backstitching ¼" inside the raw edge, sew the outside border strips to the top and bottom of the quilt, leaving an 8" overhang on each end.

8. Miter the corners. Fold the corners together diagonally, right sides together. Keep the extended border strips together and mark the mitered sewing line at a 45° angle.

9. Sew on the marked line, beginning at the corner of the quilt out to the outside edge of the border, backstitching at both ends. Trim the seam to ¼".

10. Quilt as desired.

11. Bind with 2 ½" border stripe binding strips.

Punchneedle Apron

Made by Kaye Spitzli

MATERIALS NEEDED

1 KITCHEN TOWEL

¾ YARD COORDINATING FABRIC

LIGHT WEIGHT FUSIBLE INTERFACING

BLACK PIGMA PEN

EMBROIDERY HOOP

PUNCH NEEDLE

1 STRAND LIGHTWEIGHT PERLE COTTON (SAMPLE USED #16 PRESENCIA PERLE COTTON—SEE RESOURCES, PAGE 127):

   1 SKEIN VARIEGATED LAVENDER

   1 SKEIN YELLOW

   1 SKEIN VARIEGATED GREEN

OR SUBSTITUTE 2 STRANDS EMBROIDERY FLOSS IN EACH COLOR LISTED

CLOVER GLUE FOR EMBROIDERY STITCHING TOOL (SEE RESOURCES)

SMALL EMBROIDERY SCISSORS (THOSE WITH A CURVED TIP WORK GREAT)

STITCHING INSTRUCTIONS

1. Use your kitchen towel to make an apron according to the instructions on page 110 (Sunflower apron).

2. Place the interfacing over the flower embroidery pattern on page 117. Trace 1 flower with a leaf on either side.

3. Fuse the interfacing onto the back side of the apron front, keeping the design horizontal with the apron fabric weave.

4. Place the apron in the hoop (interfacing side up), centering the flower. Keep the fabric pulled taunt in the hoop without distorting the design.

5. Thread the floss in the needle.

6. Set the needle gauge (depth of loop) to the desired setting. For Kaye's apron, the needle was set for a low loop. Follow the manufacturer's instructions, as various brands differ.

7. Your thread must lay loose, not having any 'drag' or it will pull out the stitches.

8. Place the needle where you want to start punching. Hold the needle almost perpendicular to the fabric, with the beveled side facing toward where you will punch.

9. Punch a row just inside the pattern line to outline the leaf or petal. Push the needle firmly all the way down until it stops at the base of the shank. Bring the needle back up, keeping the needle tip in contact with the fabric to avoid pulling out the loop. Drag the needle over a few threads of the apron fabric and punch again.

10. After you have made several stitches, clip the tail from the first stitch.

11. Leave a bit of space between rows when starting the next row of stitches. You will want a continuous but uncrowded line of loops on the right side of the apron.

12. When you finish an area, clip the thread before starting in a new area even if you don't change thread color. Clip and trim any longer or loose loops on the front.

13. Because the apron will be laundered regularly, Kaye recommends using Clover Embroidery Glue to permanently fix the back of the stitching.

Flower Garden Denim Shirt

Christina models the denim shirt designed and made by Peggy Claggett

MATERIALS NEEDED

DENIM SHIRT

THIS PROJECT IS A GREAT WAY TO USE UP SMALL SCRAPS.

MYLAR PIECES: 19 - ½" AND 20 - ¾"

PROJECT ASSEMBLY

Follow the instructions on pages 69-70 for making and assembling hexagons. Refer to the photo for placement.

- To make our shirt, we used:
  7 - ½" hexagons at the bottom right on side seam (a flower made of a center and 1 round).

  13 - ¾" hexagons at the shoulder (1 full flower and 1 partial that appear to overlap)

  12 - ½" hexagons spaced around the collar

  7 - ¾" hexagons above pocket (a flower made of a center and one round).

- Assemble the units, then appliqué to the denim shirt with a blind stitch. Remove the mylar pieces when just enough is left unstitched to pull them through. Stitch down the remaining opening.

Wear and enjoy the compliments!

Sunflower Apron and Towel

Apron and towel made by Shannon Slagle.

MATERIALS NEEDED

2 WOVEN COTTON KITCHEN TOWELS
COORDINATING FABRIC: 1 YARD
TWO PRINTS FOR PETALS: 8" X 16" OF EACH
FLOWER CENTERS: 4" X 8"
TEMPLATE PLASTIC: 3" X 6"

PREPARATION

Machine wash and dry the towels and fabric using detergent (not just a water dipping pre-wash) to remove fabric finishes and preshrink. Do not use fabric softener sheets when drying as they leave a residue that makes the fusible web not bond well. Iron.

CUTTING INSTRUCTIONS

COORDINATING FABRIC:

3 - 2" x width of fabric strips, cut one in half –
   you will use 2 full strips and ½ of the third strip
16 ½" by the width of the towel, plus 1"
4" by the width of the towel, plus 1"

APRON

1. Remove the bottom hem of one towel, straighten this edge if necessary. This is where you will sew on the pockets. Press.

2. On the top end of the towel, prepare the armholes of your apron. Fold the towel in half lengthwise, then draw a gradual arc starting 5 ½" out from the towel center at the top and curving toward the side 8 ½" down from the top.

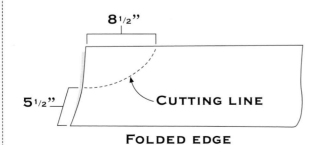

8½"

5½"

← CUTTING LINE

FOLDED EDGE

Cutting the arcs

3. Cut these arcs out of the towel.

4. Serge this cut edge.

5. Fold back approximately ¾" along these arcs to the wrong
side of the apron. Sew these edges down to make a casing to
pass the ties through.

TIES

1. Sew the 2 ½ - 2" strips together on the 2" wide ends to make
one long strip. Press.

2. Fold this strip in half lengthwise. Press.

3. Open and fold each edge into
the center and press.

4. Fold in half again and sew down both sides of the
strip to finish the edges. You now have 1 long strip.
The strip will be approximately ½" wide.

5. Finish the ends of the tie.

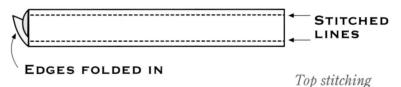

Top stitching

POCKETS ACROSS THE WIDTH OF THE BOTTOM OF THE APRON

1. Fold the 16 ½" piece of fabric in half with the fold running on
the long side. Press flat.

2. Place the folded rectangle of fabric for the
pocket on the wrong side of the apron towel.
Match the raw edge of the towel and the raw
edge of the long rectangle. The pocket fabric
should overlap your towel by ½" on each side.
Sew the towel and the pocket together. Press the seam.

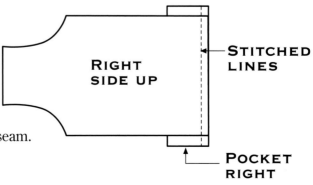

Adding the pocket

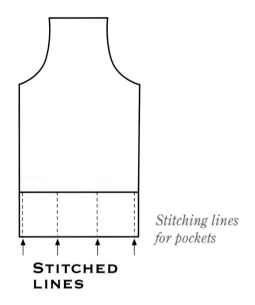

*Stitching lines
for pockets*

**STITCHED
LINES**

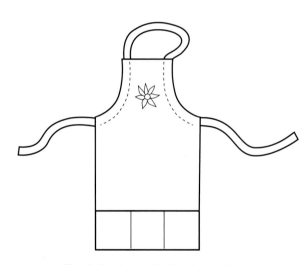

Feed tie through the channels

3. Roll the pocket fabric to the right side of the towel. Press flat.

4. Fold the edges of the ends of the pocket fabric in to leave a clean finish on the pocket edge. Sew down the ends of the pocket.

5. Determine how many pockets you would like across the bottom of the towel, usually 3 or 4. Mark these with a chalk marker. Pin in place and sew down to create the pockets.

6. Decorate the top of the apron with the sunflower appliqué.

SUNFLOWER APPLIQUÉ

1. Reduce the pattern for sunflower block on page 78 by 10%.

2. Cut the pattern for the petal on the solid line of the petal pattern.

3. Trace this pattern onto template plastic.

4. Trace this pattern 12 times onto fusible web.

5. Iron these fusible web petals onto the two fabrics that you are going to use for sunflower. Cut out.

6. Arrange on the top portion of the apron, center your appliqué approximately 3 inches from the top edge. Edges of the petals should touch. Fuse the petals to the apron.

7. Trace the center of the sunflower, using the **dashed** line as your guide, onto your fusible webbing. Iron this onto the fabric you have chosen for the center of the flower.

8. Cut this piece out on the **dashed** line. Place the center of the sunflower over the petals and fuse in place.

9. Machine appliqué with the stitch of your choice.

Feed the apron tie through one side of the apron, across the top and down the other side. Adjust the tie to fit.

Sunflower Apron and Towel

TOWEL WITH TRIM

1. Un-hem the bottom hem of the towel.

2. Fold the 4" strip in half lengthwise.

3. Place the folded rectangle of fabric for the trim on the WRONG side of the towel. Match the raw edges of the towel and the raw edge of the long rectangle. The trim fabric should overlap your towel by ½" on each side.

4. Sew the towel and the trim together along the raw edges. Press the seam.

5. Roll the trim fabric to the right side of the towel. Press flat.

6. Fold in the ends of the trim fabric to leave a clean finish on the trim edge.

7. Sew the top folded edge of the trim to the towel to seal the seam inside.

8. Sew down the edges of the trim to the towel.

9. To decorate your towel, follow the directions for sunflower appliqué on page 112. The sunflower is centered approximately 3 ½" up from the hem of the trimmed towel.

Golden in a housedress typical of the 1920s.

Laundry day at the farm.

SAMPLER SETTINGS

We have provided three options for setting your sampler blocks together. The Log Pile border setting is the least challenging of the three and makes a large throw-size quilt. The Dogwood Nine-patch and Court House Steps settings are both more challenging and make queen-size quilts.

Dogwood Nine-Patch

The Dogwood Nine-patch setting uses strip-pieced sashing, an embroidered border and an on-point nine-patch border to make a lovely queen-size quilt. We think the embroidered Dogwood blossoms add a feminine touch and make this a perfect setting for a quilt using 1930s reproductions or floral fabrics.

FABRIC REQUIREMENTS

20 SAMPLER BLOCKS

LIGHT BACKGROUND FABRIC:
   4 ½ YARDS

GREEN FABRIC: 4 ¼ YARDS

YELLOW FABRIC: 1 ½ YARDS

VARIOUS FABRICS FOR NINE-PATCH
   BLOCKS: 3" X 9" EACH OF 52
   FABRICS

BINDING: 1 YARD

CUTTING INSTRUCTIONS

FROM THE LIGHT BACKGROUND FABRIC:

27 strips 3" x wof (width of fabric) to border each block.

8 strips 5" x wof for embroidery border.

13 strips 2" x wof for nine-patches cut into 260 – 2" squares.

FROM THE GREEN FABRIC:

38 strips 1 ¼" x wof for pieced sashing.

2 strips 2" x wof for pieced sashing.

17 strips 2" x wof for final pieced border.

24 – 7 ⅝" squares cut in half diagonally twice for final pieced border (96 quarter-square triangles).

8 – 4" squares. Cut squares in half diagonally once for final pieced border (16 corner setting half-square triangles).

1 strip 6 ½" x wof for final pieced border-subcut when assembling final border.

FROM THE YELLOW FABRIC:

19 strips 2" x wof for pieced sashing.

4 strips 1 ¼" x wof for pieced sashing.

52 FABRICS FOR NINE-PATCH BLOCKS

4 – 2" squares of each fabric.

Dogwood Nine-Patch 88" x 102 1/2"

Made by Kaye Spitzli, embroidery by Arlene Lawson, quilted by Eula Lang

PIECING INSTRUCTIONS

1. Border each block with a 3" strip of the background fabric. Add the strip to the sides of the block first, then to the top and bottom.

2. If your blocks are not exactly 9" this will make them uniform; trim to 12". Blocks will finish at 11 ½".

PIECED SASHINGS

1. Make strip set units of green/yellow/green by using 34 green strips (1 ¼" x wof) and 17 yellow strips (2" x wof). Sew 1 green strip lengthwise to both sides of the yellow strips as shown in the diagram. Make 17 of these strip sets and then cut them into sets that measure 12" x 3 ½". Make 49 strip set units.

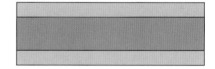

2. Assemble rows of quilt blocks by sewing a strip set unit to the right side of each block and also on the left side of the first block in each row.

3. Sew 4 blocks together per row with the sashing units. Make 5 rows.

PIECED CORNERSTONES

1. Make 2 strip set units by using 4 yellow strips (1 ¼" x wof and 2 green strips (2" x wof). Sew 1 yellow strip lengthwise on both sides of the green strip. Cut these yellow/green/yellow strip sets every 1 ¼" to make 60 units that measure 1 ¼" x 3 ½".

2. Make 2 strips set units by using 4 green strips (1 ¼" x wof) and 2 yellow strips (2" x wof). Sew 1 green strip lengthwise on both sides of the yellow strips to make 2 green/yellow/green strip set units. Cut these strips every 2" to make 30 units that measure 2" x 3 ½".

3. Sew 1 – 1 ¼" x 3 ½" yellow/green/yellow strip set to each side of the 2" x 3 ½" green/yellow/green strip set unit to make each cornerstone. Make 30 of these units.

4. Make 6 rows of horizontal sashing by sewing cornerstones between the 12" x 3 ½" strip set units from the pieced sashing instructions. Begin and end each row with a cornerstone.

5. Assemble quilt with a sashing row on top, bottom, and between each block row.

EMBROIDERY BORDER

1. Sew 5" strips together to make top and bottom borders that measure 5" x 72" and 2 side borders that are 5" x 86".

2. Trace embroidery pattern onto fabric with a pigma pen and embroider with colors of your choice.

3. Sew borders on quilt and miter corners.

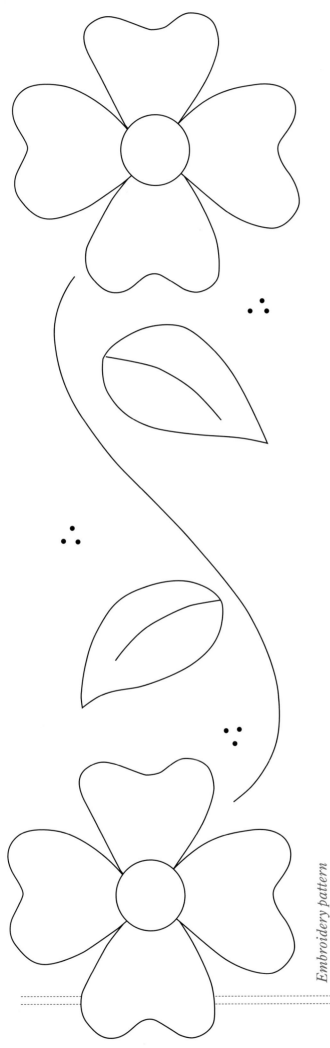

Embroidery pattern

FINAL PIECED BORDER

1. Piece together 8 green strips that are 2" x wof to make 2 side borders 85" long and top and bottom borders 73 ½" long.

2. Sew borders onto the quilt sides first, then top and bottom.

3. Nine-patches: make 52 nine-patches that are 5" square (4 ½" finished) from the 2" squares cut from the 52 different fabrics and the 260 2" white squares.

4. With the nine-patches on point, sew a 7 ⅝" quarter-square triangle to opposite sides of 44 of the nine-patch blocks.

5. Sew 2 of the 4" half-square triangles to the corners of the end nine-patches on each row. Sew the rows together using 12 of the nine-patches on each the top and bottom borders and 14 of the nine-patches on each of the side borders.

6. Sew a 6 ½" x 2" piece of green fabric (measure your quilt length and adjust this if necessary) to each end of side borders to make them measure 6 ½" x 88" (6" x 87 ½" finished).

7. Attach side pieced borders.

8. Sew a 6 ½" x 7" piece of green fabric (measure your quilt width and adjust this if necessary) to each end of the top and bottom borders to make them measure 6 ½" x 85 ½" (6" x 85" finished). Attach to the top and bottom of the quilt.

9. Piece together 5 green strips (2" x wof) to make 2 side borders that measure 100" in length. Sew to the sides of the quilt.

10. Piece together 4 green strips (2" x wof) to make top and bottom borders that measure 85 ½" in length. Sew to the top and bottom of quilt.

Wow. You've finished piecing the top.
Quilt as desired and bind.

Log Pile Border

The Log Pile setting makes a large throw. It is a perfect setting for using block scraps as the colored pieces for the Logs. This setting gives the quilt a warm cozy informal look and would be great to curl up with in front of the fireplace on a cold night!

FABRIC REQUIREMENTS

20 SAMPLER BLOCKS

BLUE TO FRAME THE 20 BLOCKS:
    2 YARDS

GREEN FOR CORNER BLOCKS, THIN
    ACCENT BORDER, AND BINDING:
    1 YARD

TAN FOR SASHING, INNER AND
    LOG PILE BORDERS: 2 ½ YARDS

ASSORTED COLORED FABRICS FOR LOG
    PILE BORDER: TOTAL OF
    1 ½ YARDS

CUTTING INSTRUCTIONS

FROM THE BLUE FABRIC:

40 – 2" x 9 ½"
40 – 2" x 12 ½"

FROM THE GREEN FABRIC:

12 – 1 ½" squares
4 – 2" x width of fabric (wof)
3 – 2" x wof
8 – 2 ¼" x wof

FROM THE TAN FABRIC:

31 – 1 ½" x 11 ¾"
4 – 1 ¼" x wof for inner side
    borders
3 – 2 ⅝" x wof for inner top and
    bottom borders

LOG PILE BORDER:

24 – 2" x 2"
52 – 2" x 3 ½"
56 – 2" x 5"
28 – 2" x 6 ½"

LOG CABIN BLOCKS:

4 – 2" squares
4 – 2" x 3 ½"
4 – 2" x 5"
4 – 2" x 6 ½"
4 – 2" x 8"

FROM ASSORTED FABRICS:
FOR LOG PILE BORDER:

24 – 2" x 6 ½"
52 – 2" x 5"
56 – 2" x 3 ½"
28 – 2" x 2"

FOR LOG CABIN BLOCKS:

4 – 2" squares
4 – 2" x 3 ½"
4 – 2" x 5"
4 – 2" x 6 ½"

QUILT ASSEMBLY

1. Sew 2" x 9 ½" blue strips to both sides of each of the 20 blocks.

2. Sew 2" x 12 ½" blue strips to top and bottom of each of the 20 blocks.

3. Centering the block in the frame, trim all the blocks to 11 ¾".

4. Lay out the blocks into 5 rows of 4 blocks each.

LOG PILE BORDER   68" x 83"   *Made by Christina DeArmond, quilted by Eula Lang*

119

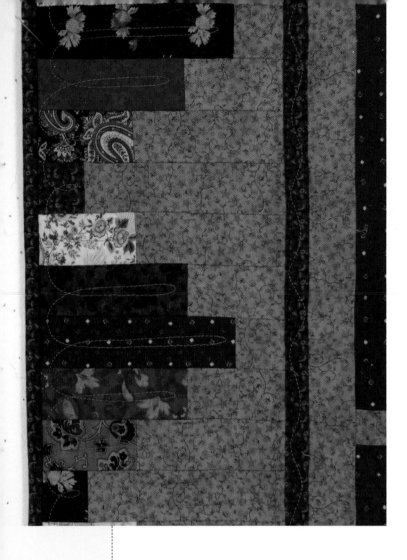

5. Sew a 1 ½" x 11 ¾" sashing strip between each of the 4 blocks for each of the 5 rows. Do not sew a sashing strip on either end of the row.

6. Assemble horizontal sashing strips by sewing a green 1 ½" square between each of 4 brown sashing strips. Repeat to make 4 strips.

7. Assemble the rows of blocks with the rows of sashing strips between them.

8. Quilt top should now measure 48 ½" x 60 ¾".

9. Inner border: from the 4 – 1 ¼" tan strips, make 2 strips 1 ¼" x 60 ¾" and sew to the sides of the quilt. From the 3 – 2 ⅝" tan strips, make 2 strips 2 ⅝" x 50" and sew to the top and bottom of the quilt. The quilt should now measure 50" x 65".

10. For the thin accent border: from the 4 – 2" green strips, make 2 strips 2" x 65" and sew to both sides of the quilt. From the 3 – 2" green strips, make 2 strips 2" x 53" and sew to the top and bottom of the quilt. Your quilt should now measure 53" x 68".

ASSEMBLING
Log Pile Border

Unit A: 2" x 2" tan square sewn to 2" x 6 ½" colored piece. Make 24.

Unit B: 2" x 3 ½" tan piece sewn to 2" x 5" colored piece. Make 52.

Unit C: 2" x 5" tan piece sewn to 2" x 3 ½" colored piece. Make 56.

Unit D: 2" x 6 ½" tan piece sewn to 2" x 2" colored piece. Make 28.

Piece together 2 strips as in the diagram for side Log Pile borders:

SIDES

Piece together 2 strips as in the diagram below for top and bottom Log Pile borders:

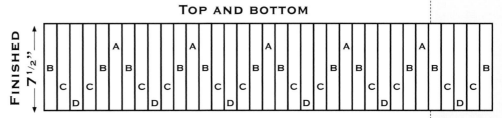

TOP AND BOTTOM

FINISHED 7½"

Log Cabin blocks for corners of Log Pile border:

Piece together 4 blocks as shown:

COLOR SCRAPS

FINAL ASSEMBLY

1. Sew the side Log Pile borders to each side of the quilt with the tan pieces touching the green border and the colored pieces toward the outside.

2. Sew a Log Cabin block to each end of the top and bottom Log Pile borders so that the tan sides will be toward the center of the quilt and the colored sides on the outer edges.

3. Sew the top and bottom Log Pile borders to the quilt with the tan pieces touching the green border and the colored pieces toward the outside.

4. Quilt your quilt, then bind with the 2 ¼" green strips.

Courthouse Steps

The Courthouse Steps setting is the most challenging of the three setting options. This is not because of sewing skill required but because of the careful attention to color placement needed to make the Courthouse Step alternate blocks. These Courthouse Step blocks visually "set each block on point" by adding a colored triangle to each side of the 18 sampler blocks. Your finished quilt will be queen-size and is a beautiful bed quilt.

FABRIC REQUIREMENTS

18 COMPLETED BLOCKS: CHOOSE YOUR FAVORITE 18 FROM THE 20 SAMPLER BLOCKS

BLUE TO FRAME THE 18 BLOCKS: 1 ½ YARDS

28 DIFFERENT PRINTS FOR THE COURTHOUSE STEP BLOCKS: ¼ YARD EACH

BEIGE FOR CENTER SQUARES, HALF BLOCKS AND INNER BEIGE BORDER: 1 ¾ YARDS

BLUE SECOND BORDER: 1 ⅛ YARDS

BEIGE PRINT FOR THIRD BORDER: ½ YARD

RED PRINT FOR OUTER BORDER AND BINDING: 3 ¼ YARDS

CUTTING INSTRUCTIONS

36 – 2" x 9 ½" blue strips for block frames.

36 – 2" x 12 ½" blue strips for block frames.

17 – 3" beige squares for the Courthouse Steps block centers.

12 – 2" x width of fabric (wof) beige strips for the half blocks and corners.

3 – 2" x wof strips from each of 28 fabrics for the 'steps'.

11 – 2" strips x wof for inner beige border.

10 – 3 ½" x wof strips from blue second border fabric.

11 – 1 ¼" x wof strips from beige print third border fabric.

4 – 6 ½" x length of fabric (lof) strips from red print outer border fabric.

4 – 2 ½" x lof strips from red print for binding.

QUILT ASSEMBLY

FRAMING THE BLOCKS

1. Sew 2" x 9 ½" blue strips to both sides of each of the 18 blocks.

2. Sew 2" x 12 ½" blue strips to the top and bottom of each of the 18 blocks.

3. Centering the block in the frame, trim all 18 blocks to 12".

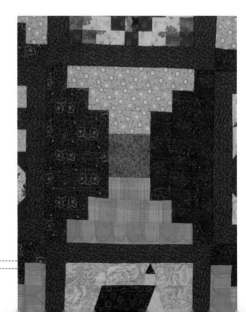

COURTHOUSE STEPS   89" x 112"   *Kaye's 1800s quilt, made by Kaye Spitzli, quilted by Eula Lang*

MAKING THE ALTERNATE COURTHOUSE STEPS BLOCKS

1. Follow the Assembly Diagram as you make your blocks so the color placement is correct. Each block uses a center square and strips of 4 different fabrics. The same fabric touches all 4 sides of each sampler block so each one of these blocks has a different color layout. We've labeled these A, B, C, and D below – notice that A, B, C and D are different fabrics and placements in EACH of the blocks. You may want to place your blocks on a design wall to more easily see the proper placement.

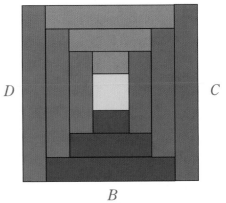

2. Use the 28 different fabrics 2" x wof strips as you sew to insure proper placement.

FOR EACH BLOCK YOU NEED:

1 – 3" beige center square
2 – 2" x 3" strips, 1 each A and B
4 – 2" x 6" strips, 1 each A, B, C and D
4 – 2" x 9" strips, 1 each A, B, C and D
2 – 2" x 12" strips, 1 each C and D

3. Sew a 2" x 3" A strip to the top of a 3" square and a 2" x 3" B strip to the bottom.

4. Sew a 2" x 6" C strip to the right side of this unit and a 2" x 6"" D strip to the left side.

5. Sew a 2" x 6" A strip to the top of this unit and a 2" x 6" B strip to the bottom.

6. Sew a 2" x 9" C strip to the right side of this unit and a 2" x 9" D strip to the left side.

7. Sew a 2" x 9" A strip to the top of this unit and a 2" x 9" B strip to the bottom.

8. Sew a 2" x 12" C strip to the right side of this unit and a 2" x 12" D strip to the left side.

9. Repeat with the 16 other blocks changing fabrics A, B, C and D for each block to coincide with correct placement in the quilt.

10. To finish the 'on point' look of the settings, make half blocks matching the fabric color surrounding the 3 sides of the block. There are 2 different half blocks used.

Courthouse Steps

HALF BLOCK A: MAKE 14

Row 1: 2" x 12" print

Row 2: 2" square beige, 2" x 9" print, 2" square beige

Row 3: 2" x 3 ½" beige, 2" x 6" print, 2" x 3 ½" beige

HALF BLOCK B: MAKE 10

Row 1: 2" square beige, 2" x 9" print, 2" square beige

Row 2: 2" x 3 ½" beige, 2" x 6" print, 2" x 3 ½" beige

Row 3: 2" x 5" beige, 2" x 3" print, 2" x 5" beige

CORNER BLOCKS: MAKE 4

Cut all pieces from the beige strips and see Assembly Diagram for placement.

1. Sew together 2 – 2" squares.

2. Sew a 2" x 3 ½" strip to the long side of this unit.

3. Sew a 2" x 3 ½" strip to the pieced side of this unit.

4. Sew a 2" x 5" strip to the side of this unit.

FINISHING

1. Sew all the blocks together into rows. Half block A will begin and end each row of half blocks on all 4 sides of the quilt center and alternate with half block B. Sew the rows together.

2. Add a beige border using the 2" beige strips.

3. Add a blue border using the 3 ½" blue strips.

4. Add a beige border using the 1 ¼" beige strips.

5. Add a red border using the 6 ½" red strips.

6. Quilt as desired.

7. Bind with 2 ½" red strips.

Assembly Diagram

About the Authors

Kaye Lawson Spitzli grew up in Eudora, Kansas with a mother, grandmother, and great-grandmother who sewed and quilted. Her sewing education began early in her childhood and there were always plenty of quilts to "dream" under, whether it be on the bed, strung over the clothesline, or still in the quilt frames in Grandma's front room. Golden was her grandmother.

Eula Scranton Lang grew up in Illinois. She too had the heritage of a mother who sewed and quilted. Eula learned to embroider as a young girl and made her first quilt when she was in junior high school. Her mom always encouraged her to sew and allowed the freedom of trial and error, no fear (thanks, Mom!).

Christina Slankard DeArmond also grew up in Eudora, Kansas. As a child, she loved to play ball, ride bicycles, roam around the creek with her brother catching ringneck snakes and basically, be a tomboy. After she married and moved to Minnesota, she took quilting classes with her friends to learn to make quilts and also to have a time of fellowship with them.

HOW WE WORK TOGETHER

Of One Mind is a group of three friends who love quilting, love having fun together and love the Lord. We chose the name based on the Bible verse, "That you may with one mind and one mouth glorify the God and Father of our Lord Jesus Christ," Romans 15:6. We also refer to our partnership as being "Three Bodies – One Brain" because we compliment each other in our gifts and talents.

We began publishing our patterns in 2002 and it takes all three of us (and three supportive husbands) to make Of One Mind work. We truly have to be able to "work" on our projects together because we share ideas and discuss dilemmas as we go (we also thoroughly enjoy spending time together).

Eula is our artist. We all come up with ideas, then Eula tries to draw what is in our heads. She is also the super achiever of the threesome, quickly finishing up her part, then trying hard to keep us on schedule for deadlines. Most of the beautiful machine quilting is done by Eula.

Kaye's family history was a rich source of inspiration.

Kaye transforms the drawings and block ideas into computer patterns. We all work on writing up the directions, then Kaye combines the directions and the diagrams to make a clear quilt pattern. Her rich family history has been a great source of inspiration.

Christina is a whiz at math, quickly notes yardages, block sizes and that "you can't put a five patch into a nine inch block." Christina also does the book work and tries to keep things organized.

Kaye, Eula and Christina are also part owners of Quilting Bits & Pieces in Eudora, Kansas. The quilt shop was established in November of 1997 and has grown considerably over the past decade. Our first-time customers are often surprised to find a quilt shop with such a large selection in such a small town (population 5,000).

RESOURCES

MYLAR PIECES
(Flower Garden Denim Shirt, page 109)
By Brandy's
www.brandysquiltpatterns.com
870-342-5005

THANGLES
(Block 3, page 23)
www.thangles.com
877-703-5284

ADD-A-QUARTER RULER
(Block 14, page 65 and Block 16, page 73)
By CM Designs, Inc.
303-841-5920

CLOVER GLUE FOR EMBROIDERY STITCHING TOOL
(Punchneedle Apron, page 108)
www.clover-usa.com

PRESENCIA PERLE COTTON
(Punchneedle Apron, page 108)
www.presenciausa.com
866-277-6364

OTHER STAR BOOKS

One Piece at a Time by Kansas City Star Books – 1999

More Kansas City Star Quilts by Kansas City Star Books – 2000

Outside the Box: Hexagon Patterns from The Kansas City Star by Edie McGinnis – 2001

Prairie Flower: A Year on the Plains by Barbara Brackman – 2001

The Sister Blocks by Edie McGinnis – 2001

Kansas City Quilt Makers by Doug Worgul – 2001

O' Glory: Americana Quilts Blocks from The Kansas City Star by Edie McGinnis – 2001

Hearts & Flowers: Hand Applique from Start to Finish by Kathy Delaney – 2002

Roads & Curves Ahead by Edie McGinnis – 2002

Celebration of American Life: Applique Patterns Honoring a Nation and Its People by Barb Adams and Alma Allen – 2002

Women of Grace & Charm: A Quilting Tribute to the Women Who Served in World War II by Barb Adams and Alma Allen – 2003

A Heartland Album: More Techniques in Hand Applique by Kathy Delaney – 2003

Quilting a Poem: Designs Inspired by America's Poets by Frances Kite and Debra Rowden – 2003

Carolyn's Paper Pieced Garden: Patterns for Miniature and Full-Sized Quilts by Carolyn Cullinan McCormick – 2003

Friendships in Bloom: Round Robin Quilts by Marjorie Nelson and Rebecca Nelson-Zerfas – 2003

Baskets of Treasures: Designs Inspired by Life Along the River by Edie McGinnis – 2003

Heart & Home: Unique American Women and the Houses that Inspire by Kathy Schmitz – 2003

Women of Design: Quilts in the Newspaper by Barbara Brackman – 2004

The Basics: An Easy Guide to Beginning Quiltmaking by Kathy Delaney – 2004

Four Block Quilts: Echoes of History, Pieced Boldly & Appliqued Freely by Terry Clothier Thompson – 2004

No Boundaries: Bringing Your Fabric Over the Edge by Edie McGinnis – 2004

Horn of Plenty for a New Century by Kathy Delaney – 2004

Quilting the Garden by Barb Adams and Alma Allen – 2004

Stars All Around Us: Quilts and Projects Inspired by a Beloved Symbol by Cherie Ralston – 2005

Quilters' Stories: Collecting History in the Heart of America by Debra Rowden – 2005

Libertyville: Where Liberty Dwells, There is My Country by Terry Clothier Thompson – 2005

Sparkling Jewels, Pearls of Wisdom by Edie McGinnis – 2005

Grapefruit Juice & Sugar by Jenifer Dick – 2005

Home Sweet Home by Barb Adams and Alma Allen – 2005

Patterns of History: The Challenge Winners by Kathy Delaney – 2005

My Quilt Stories by Debra Rowden – 2005

Quilts in Red and Green and the Women Who Made Them by Nancy Hornback and Terry Clothier Thompson – 2006

Hard Times, Splendid Quilts: A 1930s Celebration, Paper Piecing from The Kansas City Star by Carolyn Cullinan McCormick – 2006

Art Nouveau Quilts for the 21st Century by Bea Oglesby – 2006

Designer Quilts: Great Projects from Moda's Best Fabric Artists – 2006

Birds of a Feather by Barb Adams and Alma Allen – 2006

Feedsacks! Beautiful Quilts from Humble Beginnings by Edie McGinnis – 2006

Kansas Spirit: Historical Quilt Blocks and the Saga of the Sunflower State by Jeanne Poore – 2006

Bold Improvisation: Searching for African American Quilts – The Heffley Collection by Scott Heffley – 2007

The Soulful Art of African American Quilts: Nineteen Bold, Improvisational Projects by Sonie Ruffin – 2007

Alphabet Quilts: Letters for All Ages by Bea Oglesby –2007

Beyond the Basics: A Potpourri of Quiltmaking Techniques by Kathy Delaney – Fall – 2007

Borderland in Butternut and Blue: A Sampler Quilt to Recall the Civil War Along the Kansas/Missouri Border by Barbara Brackman – Fall – 2007

Come to the Fair: Quilts that Celebrate State Fair Traditions by Edie McGinnis – Fall – 2007

Cotton and Wool: Miss Jump's Farewell by Linda Brannock – Fall – 2007

You're Invited! Quilts and Homes to Inspire by Barb Adams and Alma Allen, Blackbird Designs – Fall – 2007

QUEEN BEES MYSTERIES:

Murders on Elderberry Road by Sally Goldenbaum – 2003

A Murder of Taste by Sally Goldenbaum – 2004

Murder on a Starry Night by Sally Goldenbaum – 2005

PROJECT BOOKS:

Fan Quilt Memories by Jeanne Poore – 2000

Santa's Parade of Nursery Rhymes by Jeanne Poore – 2001

As the Crow Flies by Edie McGinnis – 2007

Sweet Inspirations by Pam Manning – 2007

Quilts Through the Camera's Eye by Terry Clothier Thompson – Fall – 2007